CannaBiz

Big Business Opportunities in the New Multibillion-Dollar Marijuana Industry

Neev Tapiero

Self-Counsel Press
(a division of)
International Self-Counsel Press Ltd.
Canada   USA

Self-Counsel Press acknowledges the financial support of the Government of Canada for our publishing activities. Canadä

Printed in Canada.

First edition: 2018

Library and Archives Canada Cataloguing in Publication

Tapiero, Neev, author

CannaBiz: big business opportunities in the new multibillion dollar marijuana industry / Neev Tapiero.

(Business series)

Issued in print and electronic formats.

ISBN 978-1-77040-298-0 (softcover).—ISBN 978-1-77040-492-2 (EPUB).—ISBN 978-1-77040-493-9 (Kindle)

1. Marijuana industry—North America. 2. New business enterprises—North America. I. Title. II. Series: Self-Counsel business series

HD9019.M382N78 2018   381'.41379   C2018-901253-6
                                              C2018-901254-4

Thank you to Trina Fraser, Brazeau Seller Law for permission to use "Canadian Cannabis Legalization Highlights by Province/Territory" on the download kit included with this book. Every effort has been made to obtain permission for quoted material and illustrations. If there is an omission or error, the author and publisher would be grateful to be so informed.

Self-Counsel Press
(a division of)
International Self-Counsel Press Ltd.

Bellingham, WA   North Vancouver, BC
USA   Canada

Part 2: Business Considerations Specific to the Cannabis Industry 53

Contents

Notice to Readers

Laws are constantly changing. Every effort is made to keep this publication as current as possible. However, the author, the publisher, and the vendor of this book make no representations or warranties regarding the outcome or the use to which the information in this book is put and are not assuming any liability for any claims, losses, or damages arising out of the use of this book. The reader should not rely on the author or the publisher of this book for any professional advice. Please be sure that you have the most recent edition.

Prices, fees, and other costs mentioned in the text or shown in samples in this book probably do not reflect real costs where you live. Inflation and other factors, including geography, can cause the costs you might encounter to be much higher or even much lower than those we show. The dollar amounts shown are simply intended as representative examples.

Laws around cannabis are evolving rapidly in all jurisdictions. Please research the laws in your area and consult qualified professionals thoroughly before beginning any venture.

Dedication

To the prettiest girl with the biggest heart in the world: Dayna.

Dedicated to my son Sebastian, his mother, my amazing father and mother, grandparents, siblings, and cousins. All those who came before me; to the staff and all members at CALM, the next generation, and to the billions of victims of the War on Drugs. In the 100-year War on Drugs, yes, I believe there have been billions.

Acknowledgments

A special thank you to Ms. Johanna Metcalf for believing in me so many years ago. You helped to start something very big.

Thank you, my heroes: Emmanuelle Chriqui, June Callwood, David Hutchinson, Tommy Chong, Don Wirtshafter, Arjan Roskam, Todd McCormick, Alex Grey, Alan Young, Kirk Tousaw, Dana Larsen.

A special thank you to my departed friend Franco Loja. Strain Hunter, passionate gardener, world traveler, great friend, dreamer of peace, a rare and amazing human being. #fullgas

A special thank you to my departed friend Paul Haden. Scientist, idealist, big hearted, patient, adventurous, shaman, carnivore. One of my first teachers in life.

Another special thank you to all the staff at CALM, Dayna Heartsong, Emma Churlaud, Dora Sola, Laurence et Marcel, Solal, Elie,

Aléna Smith, Trini, Raekwon, Paul Haden, Donny Wirtshafter, Bob Erb, Joe Mandur Jr., Subcool, Olaf, Franco, Doug P, John Conroy, Solly, Gladys, Irene, Serge and Maya Chriqui, Eyal, Patricia, Zohara, Maya, Ari, Szuszi, Miriam, Pitty, Steve Isenberg, Tom Kofman and co., Ron Marzel, The Klincks, Jen Ruppert, Klaas H., Gary B., Paul Manning, Alan Young, Gavin B., Joanne "Kentucky Derby" Smail, Trini and Rae, Cynthia Pechenick, the Benisty family, the Tapiero family, the Haggerty/Freeman family, Little Thunder, Barry 001, Keat, Jim Wakeford, Steven Scorey, Jari Dvorak, Paul Rosen, Mark Zekulin, Paul Stamets, Dennis Peron, Jack Herer, Peter McWilliams, Michelle Rainey, Terence McKenna, Bob Marley, Albert Hoffman, Alex Shulgin, Jack Kerouac, Aldous Huxley, Vi Hart, @ cookiethepuppyy.

Wu-Tang is for the children.

Preface

Welcome to *CannaBiz*. I hope this book gives you a glimpse into a very new and very large world: The legal cannabis industry. No one has known legal cannabis in almost 100 years; our grandparents or great grandparents might remember. A director of Law Enforcement Against Prohibition (LEAP), a nonprofit, has called prohibition "the worst social policy since slavery." (Not a comparison, but a timeline.) Slowly but surely, that is coming to an end.

Because cannabis has been criminalized (some would say excessively) for such a long period of time it had no presence outside the black market until recently. Canada is set to become the second G7 country to legalize cannabis across the entire country, after Uruguay did it in 2014 ("Weed around the world: what legal marijuana looks like in other countries" *Global News*, 2013), which will put it at the forefront of the new industry worldwide. It is a once-in-a-lifetime opportunity for real change in social values.

My personal romance with cannabis began in the early '90s when I was in university studying for my undergraduate degree. I liked to read, among other publications, *High Times* magazines in my dorm room. Reefer madness and mandatory minimums were the policy of the day under the American Bush/Clinton/Bush administrations.

At that time, the AIDS crisis was just past its height in terms of public health issues and its stigmatization. New HIV combination therapies required individuals to consume 10 to 40 pills per day, and these pills often came with horrible side effects. Most notably was wasting syndrome, where lack of sleep and appetite were combined with a dangerously rapid loss of weight. Those with this syndrome were simply unable to absorb nutrients. Many died, not from HIV/AIDS directly but because of the symptoms related to the therapy. The same is said of other diseases such as cancer; the chemotherapy that can fight cancer can ravage the body.

In all this craziness, there was also some good; out came a story about San Francisco local named Dennis Peron who operated the first "Cannabis Buyers Club," which openly sold cannabis to those in medical need.

Other feel-good stories came out too, such as the story of Brownie Mary (Mary Jane Rathbun), who gave marijuana-laced brownies to people in the San Francisco hospices which allowed them to feel relieved of some pain and therefore able to sleep, as well as relieved of nausea so they could eat (get the munchies), which improved the quality of life for many people.

At this time I was in my early 20s. I knew the War on Drugs was a total failure; it was a misinformation campaign; there is no logical connection between prohibition and access to nonaddictive and addictive substances; and cannabis was obviously not a dangerous substance as it had a beneficial presence in my life in terms of calming my anxieties and simply helping me to experience happiness.

Add my personal experiences to the fact that cannabis can save or improve the lives of people with HIV/AIDS, cancer, MS, spinal cord injuries, and other debilitating issues, and my interest was galvanized in getting involved in this industry.

Living in Toronto, I asked around at several hemp stores in the city and not only was no one engaging in a medical cannabis movement in Toronto, no one was engaged across all of Canada. Being a true Canadian, I wrote a letter to my federal Member of Parliament, asking for changes to the criminal code to allow the use of medical cannabis.

I called Dennis Peron at his San Francisco office and asked if I could visit him and observe for a few days. I went to visit him and John Entwistle and their team during my Christmas break. They had experienced a police raid a few months earlier so sales were limited, but politically they were very busy. They turned every day into a political opportunity to make the news, respond to news stories, and counter the pundits' spin. It was very inspiring.

The medical cannabis industry in Canada, and elsewhere, was very much nonexistent, with no associations or groups, no infrastructure, no presence at all. Medical cannabis was written with quotes: "medical" marijuana or "medical marijuana." Hemp stores had to have signs saying pipes and bongs are for tobacco use only. Truly, it was in its infancy stage. It was a true pioneering experience to be among the first to change attitudes and laws around cannabis, medical or otherwise. At the time I recall the thought of saving the whales seemed more realistic.

By the time I had completed my studies, the BC Compassion Club Society (BCCCS) in Vancouver had opened its doors. About two weeks later, I had opened up Cannabis As Legitimate Medicine (later called Cannabis As Living Medicine — CALM) in Toronto with the help of James Wakeford, Jari Dvorak, and many other individuals, and a financial kickstart from Ms. Johanna Metcalfe. My own father was very leery of the legal risks I was taking, unsure my facts were accurate, but otherwise very emotionally supportive.

Over the last hundred years of prohibition, governments worldwide have not only imported the American War on Drugs philosophy into their countries, some have internalized a militant mentality to fighting drug use and abuse by legislating capital punishment, or very lengthy prison sentences for possession and/or trafficking of small amounts of cannabis. This is a testament to how backwards our national and international drug policies still are, as well as the over-politicization of the topic. A modern example of the Drug

War gone crazy is the Philippines' President Duterte's extreme approach to drug law enforcement (a Google search on this will bring up some scary stories).

Developing countries that receive international aid from the US are usually required to enforce, among other policies, the War on Drugs and require active enforcement of these issues, despite these countries often being unable to meet their higher priorities as it relates to their population's health and national prosperity. The prohibition of cannabis and enforcing the drug war is seemingly paramount.

The US has unique issues, with some states legalizing recreational marijuana while it is still illegal on the federal level. Canada has come a long way but there is still a long way to go. My hope is that this book helps us get there.

Introduction

In this book my hope is to give you an intrinsic look at an industry that captured my interest more than 20 years ago.

I have learnt it is unwise to look at the future without looking at the past. I would like to give you an overview of the current state of cannabis in comparison to past programs, while recognizing the this is an ever-changing industry on every level and by the time you read this, things may have already shifted some more.

I will give you a look at what I see, in my experience, as the best or easiest opportunities for entrepreneurs in trying to enter the industry. I hope that by reading this book, you will avoid many of the pitfalls newcomers experience.

While I saw cannabis as a viable industry back in my late twenties, at that time you could say that I had the perfect blend of fearlessness, naiveté, and a "fire in my belly" to take a chance on an uncertain and bumpy road. It was completely uncharted territory and it excited me.

Over the years the climate began to change. This was somewhat precipitated by the transformation of the industry within the US; however, different factors began to come together. Activism for legalization within Canada began to grow; people were hungry for change politically, while realizing that incarceration is a backwards approach to dealing with marijuana. Cannabis had caught the eye of corporate culture, and the understanding of how to scale up, helped create substantial revenues in legal cannabis. Interestingly, many of the people who began getting involved in the industry were people who would never have been interested in cannabis before this wave of change. Although these changes are sometimes viewed as a mixed bag in the cannabis world, it really has opened up an entire industry that is ready for business.

For many years, the forefront of the retail cannabis industry was the Netherlands with its progressive coffee shops. These coffee shops were licensed by the city of Amsterdam, and other municipalities, and not by the Dutch federal government. This was a good example of decriminalization or de-penalization without true legalization.

The next step forward was Colorado's voter initiative to legalize cannabis for adult use. Despite several federal bans, corporate money began to flow. Within a short year several multimillion-dollar corporate brands had emerged. More importantly, the corporate precedent had been set, meaning Big Cannabis (what we'll call the corporate money that is trying to take over at the moment) had its hands in the pot, so to speak.

This had a secondary effect where US foreign demands to reduce production in "source countries" began to ring hollow because the US had done such a poor job of reducing production domestically.

The next big step globally was when Canada launched its medical cannabis program, the Marihuana for Medical Purposes Regulations (MMPR). The MMPR allowed, for the first time in the world, nationwide corporate production of (medical) cannabis for mass distribution. With the experience of Colorado, private equity funds and corporate money started to position themselves and within a year or so these corporations were publicly traded. Canopy Growth Corp is now a "unicorn" status stock with valuation exceeding $1 billion near the end of 2016 more than $6 billion by end of 2017: Look at Toronto Stock Exchange stock ticker WEED.TSX.

In Canada, at the time of writing, the Access to Cannabis for Medical Purposes Regulations (ACMPR) and the *Cannabis Act* put Canada at the corporate head of legal cannabis in the world; however, it continues to be work in progress as not all sections are perfectly square with the Canadian Charter. As a result, small but important changes will happen over time.

In the US, at the time of writing, several states had legalized recreational cannabis for adults by way of voter initiative including Colorado, Washington, Oregon, Nevada, and most recently, California. A number of other states have rules around medical marijuana. The US Attorney General, Jeff Sessions, has recently rescinded the Obama-era policy of letting states govern themselves. It is completely illegal at the federal level and business basics such as tax deductions and bank services are banned. President Obama said he would not pursue legalization of cannabis but he predicted that enough states would enact it that the federal government would eventually be pressured to legalize it at the federal level. Despite the challenges, 2018 is the year California becomes the retail and entrepreneurial forefront of the worldwide cannabis industry.

The theory of evolution does not state that the strongest survive. It states that the most adaptable have the highest probability of survival. During any gold rush, only a small number of miners struck it rich. Those that prospered reliably were the people providing related services or products to the miners — tools, clothing, food, transport, lodging, etc.

There are many side businesses that will be affected by, and obtain business from, all the new ventures in the cannabis industry, as well as those businesses directly dealing with cannabis, which opens up the doors for entrepreneurs to many opportunities surrounding the cannabis industry. This could include, for a start, those in accounting, administration, advocacy, consulting, cooking, delivery, dispensaries, education, entertainment, equipment supply, extraction, genetics, growers, health care, insurance, investors, legal, marketing, sales, security, technology, testing, and more! We will cover many of these possibilities in the following chapters.

This book represents the tip of the iceberg in terms of what the future holds. The way North Americans obtain and consume cannabis will change drastically over the next two to ten years. The quality and varieties of the cannabis itself will change. An entire book or college course could be written about almost every chapter in this book. It is conceivable that several trade colleges will eventually offer two- and three-year diplomas, full degrees, or certified courses in these areas in the future. Cannabis producers will start requiring cannabis technician credentials as the industry becomes more regulated, to the benefit of the entire industry and ultimately the consumer.

Things are changing quickly, and if you are an entrepreneur with the will and the ability to get in on this industry at this time, you are at the forefront of something huge.

For more on the history of cannabis in the US and Canada, see the relevant chapters later in this book and the bonus content on the download kit.

Part 1
The Many Opportunities to Do Business in the Cannabis Industry

In taking your first steps into the business of cannabis, there are several factors to consider. Figuring out where you fit within the industry, what are you passionate about, what goals you have for yourself, and what type of work-life culture you most identify with can help get the ball rolling.

I have met people on all sides of the industry: hippies, stoners, entertainers, political activists, corporate types, opportunists, financiers, billionaires, and the homeless — you name it. Figuring out which culture you want to be a part of can be helpful in identifying where you will be most successful.

I had an academic and work background in producing theater, film, and live events. In establishing several dispensaries, I supported them with events and annual gatherings, and marketed them on social and in print media. Many skills I had prior to entering the cannabis industry were transferable but also within my field of interest and skill sets.

This was a natural fit for me, given that coming out of university I didn't see myself as going the corporate route or into a nine-to-five job. I wanted to establish my own business that I was passionate about that also served a need. It helped that it also made the world a better place.

In starting my dispensary in 1996, I became connected with the tiny but growing activist community, and was involved with patient rights, legislation, and policy activism which, surprising to me, fit much more with my personality.

I have been told many times that I have inspired people to join the cannabis industry, start their own dispensaries, or become bakers or extraction artists, in part because of the work I have done with CALM. It is a bit humbling to be at the start of something so tiny that has grown into something so massive.

It's a little bit wild west; historically, the cannabis industry has not been a place for fools or the faint of heart. We are on the precipice of the cannabis mainstream. Extreme legal risk will soon be replaced with entrepreneurs using common sense and a solid investment or financing plan.

Something to note: "Weed" is a derogatory word meaning an unwanted plant. This could not be further from the truth. Cannabis is its scientific name. "Marijuana" gets a lot of use, especially in US legal terms. As business professionals, and as advocates, avoid using "weed" and other derogatory words such as "pot," "dope," etc.

If you don't know it, learn the metric system. The cannabis industry, especially in Canada, historically uses a mix of the imperial and metric system. Buy in pounds and ounces, sell in ounces and grams. The metric system is generally easier to use because determining your kilo and gram costs is something that will soon come easily.

Keep reading and stimulate your imagination. What inspires you take your first steps in to the new cannabis industry? The cannabis industry is a much more crowded pond than in the past and I suspect that people will be jumping in for many years to come.

1
Niche Cannabis and Trends to Consider As You Begin

The cannabis industry is similar to the fashion industry. It sees trends that come in and out of style through the seasons and years. Some stay for years and some fade quickly. Some are never going away.

Matching your lifestyle to one or more of these trends is key as your love of cannabis should translate into the passion of your business.

Keep in mind that since trends come and go, if you base your business solely on a trend, you may make a lot of money for a while, but always consider the long term. How will you make money when that particular trend fades?

Similar to what happened at the emergence of the micro- or craft-brewery industry, there are niche cannabis businesses you can capitalize on:

- Greenhouse or outdoor grown cannabis

- Certified organically grown cannabis

- Cannabis imported from a specific country

- Hydroponically grown cannabis (with branded nutrients)

- Cannabis grown in a particular region such as British Columbia or in indigenous communities

- Ethically produced cannabis — without the use of animal products

- Growing or breeding specific sativa specialties, indica specialties, high-CBD specialties, kush specialties

- Celebrity branded strains and products

- Celebrity breeder (people will want to buy based on the fame of the "spokesperson" or grower)

- Growing heirloom varieties, also called landraces

- Providing pre-rolled joints

- Specializing in various or specific types of extracts, baked goods, cosmetics

- Seed production — feminized, ruderalis, high CDB, landraces

- Extracted terpenes

- Edibles — desserts, meals, capsules, infused liquids

- Infused topicals — similar to baking and cosmetics

- Strains meant to target specific symptoms such as sleeplessness and spasms or diseases such as cancer and multiple sclerosis

These are but a few possibilities of many in the cannabis industry. You are only limited by your imagination, passion, and investment size.

Again, the cannabis trade goes through trends like any industry. What's popular or valuable today is boring in a year or two, perhaps longer. Here are some examples of current trends as of the writing of this book:

- Kush strains are more valuable than other strains despite yielding less than other premium strains.

- LED lighting systems hold much promise in delivering next generation, high-quality lighting with very little heat produced — they have yet to fully replace LED lights industry-wide.

- The cannabis industry employs chocolate and candy marketing strategies.

- Electronic ballasts — component for high-intensity light that produces less heat than traditional magnetic ballasts.

- Juicing of fresh cannabis plants.

- Terpene extraction.

- Distillates.

- High CBD products.

- Dabbing — consuming extracts using a chef torch and a glass bong, called a rig (butane hash oil extraction).

- Phoenix Tears (heptane extract) supposedly "cures cancer." Be very careful with any medical claims and read Chapter 15 on Drug Identification Numbers (DINs).

- Landrace strains — hunting for and retrieving untouched seed stock from its native environment. See some landrace adventures at strainhunters.com. They are also known as heirloom strains.

- Vaporizers and vaporizer pens — devices that heat cannabis, or cannabis extract, without combustion for easy, discreet inhalation of vapors. Most vaporizers are designed for consuming extracts only, or plant matter only.

Being tuned in to the culture around cannabis will provide valuable insight into long-term strategies.

A reputation for high-quality reliable service, products, or strains is really the best marketing. It will set you apart from your competitors as well as from Big Cannabis. You do not need to be the grower of the niche cannabis to be known as the go-to person for reliable sources or services, so long as you find your niche and become really good at doing what you do.

Niche cannabis products are also a hedge against corporate dominance. After a trend has lasted several years, it will likely fade or fall into the mainstream of retail cannabis. Finding new and emerging trends, being flexible, and staying ahead of the curve is key to longevity in this industry.

If you think of the number and variety of micro- and craft-brewed beers and the hundreds of related services, you will understand the vastness of these uncharted opportunities.

2
Micro-Production Licenses

While things are very different between the US and Canada in terms of the cannabis industry, it is exciting to note that in November of 2017 Health Canada announced that it would launch a program to approve micro-production licenses. This presents potentially amazing opportunities to enter the craft production industry in Canada.

The current cost to get a building approved as a fully Licensed Producer (LP) will cost $2 to $10 million CAD and there could be a two- to five-year waiting period, not including the time and cost of obtaining a building first.

By reducing the costs and barriers to entry with micro-producer licenses, Health Canada wants to reduce — or end — the presence of the black or gray cannabis market as part of the legalization program.

This could represent the single best entrepreneurial opportunity I can see at the time of writing, if Health Canada executes this program properly and quickly. It is also in its infancy stage so critical components are not known.

The new micro-producers' licenses will be subdivided into the following:

- Micro-cultivation: producing cannabis

- Nursery license: producing seeds and clones

- Micro-processing: extraction and refinement

These three micro-producers can only sell their product to licensed processors or authorized researchers.

- Industrial hemp: sell whole plants with less than 0.3 percent THC to the public

Health Canada is in the process of public consultation and could have an application process in place by the summer of 2018, but this is all up in the air as of this writing.

This represents a substantial change to the future of craft cannabis production. As of June 2017, there were almost 7,000 personal or designated production licenses and thousands more of unlicensed grow ops. It is unknown how many of them are personal production only or involved in diversion of the black or gray market.

Some of what is not known about the micro-processor license as of this writing:

- How much administration is required to obtain a micro-production license?

- How long is the processing time?

- What are the minimum or maximum space, power, and security requirements?

- What is the distinction between micro-producer and licensed producer? Square footage? Annual sales?

- How many micro-production licenses does Health Canada have in mind or will it approve? How much time will it take for approval?

- What is the process of approval? RCMP security checks will be in place.

- What is the additional effort and cost associated with compliance and analysis?

- How will micro-producers work with LPs, or provincial and territorial partners?

These are all important factors to consider if you want to pursue a micro-production license in Canada.

One of the biggest challenges craft growers will face is adherence to quality assurance (QA) processes, and making sure someone is in charge of QA and legal requirements.

Historically, craft producers have been lone wolves, in that they worked alone or with one or two other partners maximum. Secrecy was paramount. Being a jack of all trades was a requirement as you would need to be proficient at such things as carpentry, electrical, air conditioning, on top of growing. This will now all change because the key to greater success is to have people who excel in their areas contribute to the cause, and making sure you follow the rules.

There is probably room for lone wolves who produce a specific quality and strain in limited quantities provided they can comply with various ACMPR requirements. (For more information on the ACMPR visit HealthCanada.gc.ca/mma, and refer to Chapter 26 as well.)

In order for these types to succeed, they must learn to work in a team environment with proper documentation, following standard operating procedures — not easy for these individuals as they honed a mentality away from these skills.

In the case of a highly skilled grower, or grow master, the team must take their cues or orders from the grower. After many years of honing their craft, it is the grower's job to reproduce his or her methods and quality on a larger scale. Compliance and administration for a lone wolf may challenging at first as it was never part of his or her skill set.

In the US, production is related to each state's medical or recreational marijuana program, however, the application process in each state at the time of writing is less stringent than Health Canada standards.

3
Doctors, Pharmacists, and Nurse-Practitioners

If you are interested in the medical side of the cannabis industry, then you should first study how the clinics do business. Doctors are the gatekeepers of the medical program in that they must sign the required Health Canada or state-required forms. Nurse practitioners are allowed to sign forms in certain provinces and territories and remote regions. Dentists are also allowed to sign ACMPR documents as long as the patient presents a dentistry-related issue for which cannabis is considered beneficial. Since the beginning of Health Canada's Marihuana for Medical Purposes Regulations (MMPR) in July 2013, clinics have demonstrated that cannabis medicine can be a viable business.

Most small clinics are managed by individuals who are owners or co-owners and, in the case of cannabis medicine, the doctor is rarely an owner of the clinic. This creates a buffer between physician compensation — over and above provincial healthcare billing — and the source of revenue, the licensed producers themselves who wish to acquire medical users as part of the services they wish to provide.

Most doctors in Canada will not sign a prescription form for medical cannabis for a number of reasons, primarily because there is not enough research on cannabis to prescribe it at the treatment level, or because some of them may have an aversion to liability-related issues — which is normal among professionals. Physicians, from what I've seen, are largely unwilling gatekeepers of the Health Canada medical cannabis programs, the Medical Marijuana Access Regulations (MMAR), MMPR, and its most recent program, the Access to Cannabis for Medical Purposes Regulations (ACMPR). Less than 1 percent of Canadian doctors have signed the ACMPR documents.

Because of Canada's socialist healthcare system, physicians are only supposed to obtain revenue in the form of provincial health-care billing. Health Canada Licensed Producers (LPs) cannot pay physicians directly or indirectly for prescribing products. It is also illegal for physicians to suggest or to funnel patients to any specific LP. This represents an administrative hurdle for LPs wishing to work with doctors for the purpose of obtaining new clients/patients.

Doctors work for the clinics that provide medical licenses, although direct commissions and royalties are not permitted. Education or administrative fees are usually paid for by the LP. There are fewer conflicts of interest if the physician has no ownership in the clinic or its business dealings.

It's been my experience that doctors in Canada expect to earn $1,000 per day or more, depending on what specialist credentials they may have. Pharmacists expect $50 to $100 per hour. Nurse-practitioners expect about $75 to $300 per hour. These rates will vary greatly depending on where you are located and what is expected of your healthcare practitioner, specifically what's in his or her job description.

Clinics may or may not provide primary care in order to provide a diagnosis and prescription. Attracting pre-diagnosed clients means obtaining medical documents from the applicant ahead of time and vetting them for content and authenticity. The documents must pass two tests: Do the medical documents support the application and diagnosis adequately? Are the documents authentic? More serious diagnoses often pass these tests more easily than less serious diagnoses. Offering or not offering primary care are two entirely different business models. Your healthcare practitioner may or may not be interested in pursuing primary care opportunities.

It is highly possible that healthcare practitioners that engage in the ACMPR inappropriately will draw some or every Provincial College's scrutiny. Any criminal charges or negative repercussions by the physician will reflect poorly on the Provincial College, whether small or large, will likely result in your current healthcare practitioner quitting your clinic and you will have a very difficult time hiring new physicians in the future because your business plan has put a physician's license in jeopardy.

Primary care is simply a general practitioner who takes on patients for the long term in the capacity of providing primary care services such as annual physical checkups, physical complaints, requests for lab tests, referrals to specialists, and prescribing drugs to be filled at the pharmacy. Not all general practitioners will provide primary care. Specialists almost never provide primary care. If you are not sure and require primary services, ask the clinic in your area.

At this point, several years after the MMPR/ACMPR corporatized medical cannabis, I would not advise investing in a clinic as a standalone business. The field is already crowded with established and branded clinics. I believe it would only be feasible under unique circumstances and with unique partners.

In the individual US states there could be an exception to this standalone model if —

- that state is allowing for a wide range of cannabis products,

- that state is allowing for a wide range of diagnoses to qualify,

- that state is allowing for cultivation and storefronts,

- you have preexisting relationships with hundreds or thousands of residents of that state who would qualify, or

- that state is enacting a medical or recreational law where previously none had existed

If you are thinking of pursuing this clinic opportunity, expect competition, from established businesses and brands, from states that have already medicalized. It is easier to partner with an established brand if you can demonstrate strong conversions of residents to join the medical program.

4.

Clones, Tissue Cultures, and Seeds

Clones, tissue cultures, and seeds represent the bulk of work in the propagation of cannabis plants. Although the equipment required is not generally expensive to buy, dealing with each item requires different equipment, moderate experience and some skill. Finding your niche in one of these specialties could be the key to your cannabis business.

Retailing or wholesaling clones requires you obtain necessary licenses from Health Canada in Canada, or your individual state in the US. The license in Canada would only allow you to wholesale or retail genetics to licensed producers, analysts, and authorized producers. It is not clear, at this point, if you would legally be allowed to sell genetics to the general public. In the US, the state licenses may or may not allow you to sell genetics to the general public, depending on the state (and the fluctuating state of things at the moment).

1. Clones

Clones are rooted branches taken from a sexed (female) mother plant and placed in a high humidity environment; also called "clips" or "cuttings." Clones are genetically identical to their mother plants. Smaller LPs will need constant and regular access to high-quality clones; they should be well rooted, at least six inches tall, healthy green in color, mold-free and pest-free in one-inch rock-wool, oasis cube, or peat pot.

It is critical to the success of your future business, and to your reputation, that every clone is bug and pest free. Good analysis should support your confidence in marketing your products and services.

Clones need to be transplanted shortly after roots appear. They can be ready for sale 7 to 20 days from clipping. Two or three weeks after this point, they will start to show signs of stress and deteriorate. Lowering the temperature (refrigeration) of the rooted clones extends the shelf life a few days longer. They are relatively cheap to make, but require specific gardening skills and the right environment and equipment. Time-wise, they require two three-minute visits per tray every single day until rooted. Some gardeners believe you should leave unrooted clones in rockwool for ten days undisturbed. Cannabis gardening can be an art/science/craft/trade as demonstrated by this one simple function.

Having many clones and many types of clones will be an in-valuable service. Clones can cost pennies to make and may retail for between $2 and $20 each in Canada and the US. Sometimes prices can be higher if it is a coveted or rare strain. Knowing your client base will help you avoid having clones go to waste and maxi-mize on seasonal opportunities.

When shipping, do not expose young plants to 12 hours of dark-ness or the flowering cycle may start. Using a simple AAA battery operated set of LEDs inside any packaging will keep that from hap-pening. Obtaining clones for personal medical production used to be a matter of networking and paying $1 to $5 per clone depending on various factors. There were no guarantees that genetics were accurate, plants were pest-free, or that they were even female. Although legalization should end this, it is conceivable that microprocessors will have to add QA analysis, and proper documentation to each clone on each order which could drive up the cost of clones dramatically.

2. Tissue Cultures

Tissue culture is similar to cloning with the added feature that you can collect 5 to 20 times the number of tissue cultures versus the number of clones. The process requires a small but dedicated lab space and a qualified and experienced technician. Proper, super-cool storage can extend storage for many years. Qualification could come in the form of one or two years of biochemistry studies, or by becoming a college-certified lab technician.

By meticulously taking rice-sized plant samples and growing them in sterile agar and hormones, you may yield a healthy four-inch clone in about six weeks. They can be grown in compact test tube containers and shipped nationwide in Canada, and statewide where legal. When shipping, do not expose young plants to 12 hours of darkness or the flowering cycle may start.

However, the upfront costs suggest that the tissue culture business, while potentially lucrative, should be avoided unless you already have moderate or advanced-related skills and have many required laboratory components in place, such as dedicated laboratory space, sterile air hood, incubator, petri dishes, agar, and related compounds. There are off-the-shelf tissue culture kits for sale but these are better suited for hobbyists.

Tissue cultures need to be transplanted no more than two weeks after they have established in the test tubes or they will start to show signs of stress. Like clones, lowering the temperature after rooting can extend the shelf life a few days.

Tissue cultures is the most complicated and expensive of the three options discussed in this chapter. However, it will require the least amount of space. There are many books and videos that will help you get up and running. I have seen several free online courses on YouTube. Although none of the courses themselves focus on cannabis only the publicly available reference information exists and is disseminated via these online courses. There are many short videos on YouTube regarding cannabis and tissue culture.

The user "Microclone" on YouTube has several short instructional videos that demonstrate the tissue culture process.

3. Seeds

Seed production and seed breeding is a required part of any large agricultural project.

Involving other LPs testing your seed stock will be highly useful for both parties if done properly. Your reputation will dictate other LPs' eagerness or willingness to test-market your seeds.

If your seeds can win competitions such as the Cannabis Cup in Amsterdam; San Bernardino, California; or Denver, Colorado (visit www.cannabiscup.com for more information), for example, they will acquire a great reputation and actual pedigree. They will therefore be worth more.

Expect about half of your expenses to go to marketing. Seed production virtually costs pennies to produce and can retail from $1 to $30 for each seed, sometimes higher. Seeds are generally more vigorous than clones.

Seeds may be legal or a "gray area" in many countries, so consult a local government representative and lawyer in each country before proceeding or considering business there. Research other, larger seed banks in Canada, the US, and elsewhere. You will start to see trends and discover why some seeds are more expensive than others.

Robert Connell Clarke's book *Marijuana Botany* (Ronin Publishing, 1981) is a good place to start to learn about breeding. Jorge Cervantes has an excellent book on general cultivation called *Marijuana Grow Basics* (Van Patten, 2009), also supported with YouTube instructional videos. See the Resources section on the download kit included with this book for more information.

Historically there has been a market for retail seed banks which can do well in large urban areas as part of the tourism industry or mail order only. It is not clear if this will be legal under the *Cannabis Act*.

In the US, seeds are illegal at the federal level and probably illegal at the state level unless it is specifically included as part of a voter initiative. It is probably illegal to cross state lines with viable cannabis seeds as well to export them outside the US.

Inventory start-up costs for a seed bank can be as low as $15,000 to $20,000 in my estimation — this does not include cost of marketing, web development, or legal costs. As an online store, most of your start-up cost is in inventory and marketing. Knowing what strains and what seed companies to buy from, and what your customers will want is a matter of experience. Before you invest in inventory, ask yourself a few questions:

- Which seed suppliers are reputable?

- Which strains are popular?

- Which strains are new?

- Which seed companies have won awards? Won recently?

- What seeds do people want that are feminized or ruderalis or both?

- Which strains have a short flowering cycle? Or long flowering cycle?

- Which strains are more pest resistant?

- What is your online marketing strategy?

- Do any seed banks have marketing materials to assist you in promotions?

5
Control Standards
When Growing

1. Analyses

Regardless of which country you live in, whether recreational or medical settings, each lot of legally grown cannabis needs to be analyzed for many facets including THC, CBD, microbes, pesticides, and heavy metals.

Under the Canadian ACMPR all Licensed Producers (LPs), even small producers, will need to have each lot and strain of cannabis tested for these five different sets of required analyses. An LP may require at least five or more tests for every strain — four to six times per year per strain. As the number of producers increases, more labs will have to be set up to accommodate the industry's needs. Larger, well-funded LPs will likely have an analysis lab within their own facilities.

Providing analyses as a service to other LPs is a large administrative endeavor with many substantial responsibilities. The analyst in charge will need to be experienced in dealing with Health Canada, properly qualified/certified, and extremely well organized. Analysis equipment can be very costly and it will need to be regularly calibrated using established standards and protocols. High Performance Liquid Chromatography is the likely standard for most analysis requirements.

LPs will likely want their analysis to be as local as possible; however, LPs will ship cross country if needed to a lab that complies with Health Canada Good Lab Practices (GLP) and provides competitive services.

There are many types of analysis equipment available. You should familiarize yourself with each one regarding a cost-benefit analysis for each piece. Retail prices for analytic services can vary anywhere from a few dollars to hundreds or thousands of dollars per analysis. Bulk purchase of analyses will likely lower costs. Setting up a proper lab will start around $300,000 to $800,000 CAD, depending on how new the equipment is and the scale of the operation — it could be substantially higher.

Off-the-shelf home analysis kits are not certifiably acceptable, especially if they do not employ the use of proper standards (see section 1.1 for more on that). They could be useful in producing crude but useful data and reducing the overall costs of official or certified analysis.

The specialist who calibrates the equipment may not be the analyst in charge. Analysts must adhere to strict Quality Assurance (QA) standards and Good Laboratory Practices (GLP) in compliance with Health Canada standards. Analysts must differentiate between certifying a sample versus certifying an entire lot or harvest. Your analyst and QA and Responsible Person-in-Charge (RPIC) will negotiate these details.

Copies of all final analyses must be sent to Health Canada as part of the QA process which includes compliance, liability, and record-keeping. A sample of each batch must be stored for two years minimum by the producer.

There are five main classes of cannabinoids: CBC, CBD, CBG, CBN, and THC. Health Canada does not require a full cannabinoid profile; however, labeling is limited to THC and CBD. Big Pharma and Big Cannabis will tend to focus on these two cannabinoids as well. Further study of lesser known cannabinoids (and therapeutic terpenes) will likely yield promising results. Your analyst should have several options depending on what your end goals are.

No matter which country you wish to do business in, consult with a biochemist for a greater understanding of opportunities within the field of analysis and lesser known cannabinoids. Being an analyst for several producers would provide you with valuable information on the inner workings and long-term goals of your clients.

1.1 Control standards for analyses

One of the requirements for proper analysis is access to pure (99.9 percent or better) individual cannabinoids, also known as control standards or simply "standards." Comparing plant samples to each standard will determine necessary values (called an "assay") required for compliance and labeling.

Where these standards are obtained is critical. LPs now produce their own in Canada. Outside of Canada most foreign governments, and some bio-corporations or universities, make their own standards in compliance with their high-risk narcotic production regimes. Each entity may have separate methods of obtaining those standards. Purity standards and methodology will vary slightly from producer to producer and jurisdiction to jurisdiction.

While it may seem insignificant, a high degree of analytical accuracy is the cornerstone of any serious agricultural project. The ACMPR should herald a new generation of affordable industry approved standards and testing, taking much of the guesswork out of the growing and breeding processes.

Most biochemists will tell you analysis is everything. This is because proper analysis will provide a critical navigational guide; it tells a producer how to make product better, or different, or even if a strain is worth developing at all. Analysis early in a grow cycle may save you the aggravation of destroying otherwise high-quality cannabis that does not pass analysis.

A further axiom biochemists will tell you is "sample preparation is everything."

In Canada, you will need to create a full product information sheet (PIS) for each strain that is consistent from batch to batch. See Health Canada's website for further details and for a full example of a PIS. Although tedious, you will need to pass every PIS test.

In the US, check with each state for details on what tests need to be passed; since cannabis is illegal federally and allowed only by certain states, the rules can be different.

2. Batch Sampling Your Analyses

As a successful cannabis producer, not only do you require reliable analysis, you will need to know how reliably accurate your own analyses really are. It is common practice to send duplicate samples (1 to 2 percent of all samples) to a secondary lab. The lab results should be identical to your own results. If there is any variation, someone on your team needs to understand exactly why and what it means in the long term. If there is a large discrepancy in results, then you have identified a serious business issue.

Health Canada keeps a list of labs on its cannabis website: healthcanada.gc.ca/mma.

Consult your state health department at the state level for any rules around labs in the US.

Beneficial Insects and Natural Pest Control

Natural pest control presents opportunities for entrepreneurs in parts of the US where it is legal at the state level, and across all of Canada. It could also be a viable opportunity outside the cannabis industry; for example, the food service industry needs pest control, so the market for finding clients is bigger than just the cannabis industry.

All dried cannabis must be absent of any pesticides. The AC-MPR makes the need for pest control without pesticides obvious. Predator mites, nematodes, ladybugs, and other beneficial insects or other natural pest control can be very effective in controlling pests on cannabis plants, especially if applied preventively.

Prompt delivery of beneficial insects is critical. There are only a small number of companies in Canada currently providing this type of service. The space and start-up requirements could be small if done well.

Here is a quick guide to some pests that are of concern to the cannabis industry:

- Spider mites are the primary pest in regards to cannabis production. They are tiny spider-like creatures that can only be seen under magnification. There are also several subspecies. They reproduce quickly and can devastate a crop with their eggs and webs. Furthermore they can linger for weeks or months after a room and crop has been finished and "cleaned up." They live primarily in the under foliage of the plant. Common treatment can include various species of predator mites.

- Aphids are sap-sucking, highly reproductive bugs. They come in various colors and have telltale "tail pipes" at the rear of their abdomen. Common treatment for aphids can include introducing ladybugs, parasitic wasps, or both.

- Adult fungus gnats are small, flying, mosquito-like bugs. Their larvae live in moist, dark environments such as soil. They injure and feed off roots which expose the plant to other deadly pathogens. Common treatments include adding nematodes, which look like microscopic worms, to the feed water.

There are many types of pests that require short- and long-term remediation. There could be many options to treat each pest, and learning what to do often requires years of experience and note taking.

Consult an entomologist for a greater understanding of this opportunity. Universities with entomology departments are very good sources of information and qualified labor. It is an easy selling point to growers to constantly have some form beneficial insects in production gardens at all times.

One company has online options: www.naturalinsectcontrol. com/.

You can use most search engines using the terms "natural pest control" and "beneficial insects" (your state/province) and you should be able to find local resources.

7
Edibles, Topicals, Extracts, Capsules, Concentrates

1. Edibles, Topicals, and Extracts

Edibles, topicals, and extracts, including tinctures, balms, baked goods, and capsules are ideal for the cottage industry and for small and craft producers because they require very little space and training. They also make up the bulk of the cottage cannabis industry.

Hygienic food handling procedures are a must. Some municipalities have certification training for safe food handling. Some municipalities provide training and testing online. Consult a lawyer before production begins as provincial, state, and federal policy and law are in a constant state of flux when it comes to cannabis businesses.

1.1 Need to know: Cannabinoids as the basis of concentrates and extracts

High-quality grown cannabis will produce flowers. Tiny sparkly crystal-type structures appear on the flora clusters and less so on the leaves and stalk. The stalk of this structure is called a non-glandular trichome and is composed of many therapeutic compounds called cannabinoids. On top of the stalk is a spherical structure composed mostly of THC. It is called the glandular trichome; these are commomly referred to as "trikes." There are several classes of cannabinoids, each class expresses minor variations in their chemical structure. The classes we know of include THC, CBD, CBC, CBA, and CBG.

While each cannabinoid has one or more therapeutic value, much of the science points to the fact that different mixes of cannabinoids can produce different therapeutic effects, sometimes with drastic differences.

Cannabinoids are usually alcohol-soluble or fat-soluble compounds and this forms the basis of almost all concentrates and extracts. Dosing information is always critical. Whenever you make your own products for sale, it is vital to record and log the weight and quality of the cannabis used. Methodology and full ingredients lists should be available on request. Consistency in potency from batch to batch is critical to your brand.

The basic equation for dosage is weight of cannabis used divided by the total volume of liquid after extracting the plant matter. The result should be expressed in hundreds of mg per unit (units for such products as a cookie or lollipop). It will be difficult to extract all the liquids.

Microdosing cannabis — consuming tiny amounts of cannabis, cannabis extract, or high CBD product — is an increasingly popular trend and typically uses approximately 10 to 50 mg per dose.

2. Tinctures

Making tinctures is a very old method of producing plant medicines. It is common to soak the plant matter in a high-grade alcohol or grain alcohol for one to two weeks and store in a dark, cool room. Filter out the plant matter with cheesecloth and again with a vegetable press, collecting the valuable liquid. A grape press can also be used for making larger batches. Batches can be divided into eye dropper bottles for retailing.

Note: Never ingest high-grade grain alcohol directly — even in drop form as it will burn the tissues in your mouth and on your tongue. Tinctures can work faster than ingestion because alcohol is absorbed by the body into the bloodstream before entering the small intestine. They are ideal for people who have digestion issues as they bypass the digestion process.

Alcohol and cannabis together has an unpleasant taste; adding sweeteners or other herbs can be beneficial. I have also seen tinctures that are mixed with various herbs. Some examples are mint, thyme, St. John's Wort, dandelion, chamomile, sage, stevia, garlic, and even hot peppers.

Consult with a herbalist for proper hygienic standards, techniques, labeling, and access to high-grade grain alcohol. A herbalist can also be helpful in employing other herbs if you choose to do so.

Dragon Elixir is a good example of a brand of tinctures with different recipes targeting various medical symptoms.

3. Balms

Balms are for dermal (skin) applications and provide localized relief to targeted areas such as an arthritic joint or sore back. It is also a good option for people who cannot or do not want to smoke or eat cannabis.

Similar to making tinctures, you can soak cannabis plant matter in oil for several days then filter out the plant matter with cheesecloth or a vegetable/grape press. Use an oil with a long shelf life like olive, corn, vegetable, or coconut. Add this infused oil to melted beeswax and pour into its final container and let cool. I would start with a half oil and half beeswax recipe. The final product should have the consistency of lip balm.

If your final product is too soft or oily, you can melt it down again and add more beeswax. If it is too hard, melt it down again and add more oil — infused or otherwise. Balms can be made with many other ingredients such as coconut oil, shea butter, or cocoa butter. You can also add tiny amounts of essential oils for complementary aromas. Keep and store notes on each batch for proper labeling. (Again, never put essential oils in pure form directly on skin and don't ingest them!)

It is difficult to consume too much cannabis via dermal transmission; however, dosing information and ingredients should always be included on packaging.

4. Extracts

Extracts come in different forms and require diverse methods of production and expertise. Extensive literature on each of these methods is readily available, as are discussion groups, and many useful instructional videos on YouTube. Listed are some of the types of extracts made from high- or low-grade cannabis:

- Bubble: Made using ice water and several silk screens to catch the tiny glandular trichomes that can be agitated off the plant matter. Some people use dry ice (frozen CO_2).

- Butane Hash Oil (BHO) is made by passing butane ($C4H10$) through a canister of ground cannabis. Making BHO can be very dangerous. People have died. Do not attempt without a properly licensed laboratory. It must be fully purged of hydrocarbons (below detectable levels) using a vacuum purging machine.

- Budda: Pronounced BUH-DAH, it is similar to BHO with further aerating refinements. This creates a crumbly sticky white-yellowish powder. This tends to have the highest concentration of cannabinoids and fetches high retail prices. It can oxidize into red or green or darker colors.

- Iso: Made using isopropanol, or isopropyl alcohol. The end result is a black or dark tarry substance. While potent, it usually contains high amounts of unpalatable chlorophyll.

- Phoenix Tears: The process is similar to Iso, but using heptane (camping fuel) instead of isopropanol. Also can be dangerous to make. Do not attempt without proper equipment and certification. Only use laboratory grade solvents (very pure) and they must be fully purged of hydrocarbons.

Table 1
Terpene Chart

Terpene	Benefit	Aroma
Pinene also found in pine needles	Anti-inflammatory Antibacterial Bronchodilator Aids memory	Pine Earth
Myrcene also found in hops and mangoes	Sedative Sleep aid Muscle relaxant	Floral Pungent Earth
Limonene also found in citrus and mangoes	Acid reflux Antianxiety Antidepressant	Citrus Fresh spice
Terpinolene also found in coriander	Analgesic Pain reduction Digestion and stomach	Pine Herbal Anise Lime
Linalool also found in lavender	Anesthetic Analgesic Anticonvulsive Antianxiety	Flowers Lavender Citrus Fresh spice
Terpineol also found in mugwort	Calming aid Antibacterial Antiviral Immune-system booster	Lilac Citrus Wood
Caryophyllene also found in black pepper	Anti-inflammatory Analgesic Protects cell lining Digestive tract	Citrus Spice
Humulene also found in basil	Anti-inflammatory	Robust Herbaceous Earth
Ocimene also found in thyme and alfalfa	Decongestant Antiseptic Antiviral Bactericidal	Citrusy green Wood Tropical fruit

Table 2
Hydrocarbons

Number of carbons	Molecule	Name	Melting Point in Celsius	Common name or reference
1	C1H4	Methane	-182	A greenhouse gas
2	C2H6	Ethane	-183	Used in antifreeze
3	C3H8	Propane	-187	BBQ gas
4	C4H10	Butane	-138	Lighter fluid
5	C5H12	Pentane	-129	Component of polystyrene foam
6	C6H14	Hexane	-95	Component of glue and roofing products
7	C7H16	Heptane	-90	Camping fuel
8	C8H18	Octane	-56	A component of jet fuel
9	C9H20	Nonane	-53	Used in organic solvents
10	C10H22	Decane	-29	A component of gasoline

- Honey Oil: A clear, thick, sticky substance usually made with butane or similar hydrocarbon (e.g., propane, pentane, hexane, heptane, or octane) for the extraction process. It is sometimes tinted yellow or red, depending on the process. You should be able to see clearly through a glass container full of it and it will pour slowly like melted glass; the slower it pours the better. This is a very high-quality product but must be fully purged of hydrocarbons, below detection levels. Do not attempt without proper equipment and certification. Only use laboratory grade solvents (very pure) and not off- the-shelf butane.

- Rosin: Dried or fresh plant matter is pressed between two hot plates until a resin emerges which is collected, dried, and then consumed like hash or budda. Specific pressure and temperature is key.

- Distillate: Much like water distillation, cannabis plant matter or extract is heated to a specific temperature where THC vaporizes. This vapor is cooled down and condenses then collected in a separate container. Other cannabinoids and terpenes can be extracted at different temperatures using this method.

- Terpenes: Terpenes are specific molecules associated with smell or flavor. Terpenes can be extracted from several plants including cannabis, mango, lavender, hops, lemons. Terpenes and terpene production are legal in Canada. Therapeutic terpenes are a largely understudied facet of cannabis and medicine in general. See Table 1 for a terpene chart.

Extracts tend to yield between 1 and 10 percent return: for every 100 grams of whole cannabis, expect one to ten grams of extract in return for most extracts. Even less with terpene extraction. Higher quality cannabis will increase the overall quality of the cannabis product but may or may not increase your yield.

5. Baked Goods

You can put most extracts into a cookie, brownie, pesto, or any high-fat-content food product. Many recipes and instructions exist online for all kinds of foods and desserts. Masking the taste of cannabis is difficult without using extracts. You will however, maximize your potency by using whole ground cannabis in your recipe, which may be less palatable.

Browned cannabis, while not very palatable, can be used to make edibles such as pesto or oatmeal cookies.

When marketing an edible item, always provide an ingredients list and dosing information, whether it is required or not. Each item or unit should contain between one to two grams of whole cannabis — or its equivalent in extracts. Maximum retail price for a two-gram item tends to be $8 to $20 (around the same prices in Canada and the US).

An attractive sticker or packaging on each item is great for branding. Baked goods tend to retail for double the bakers' wholesale price. Always include ingredients list and dosing information.

Dosing information is not required in all jurisdictions (yet) but it is responsible canna-baking behavior. Be sure to research the laws in your area. For example, in Colorado there are strict rules on labeling packaging and dosing, including:

- Limit of 10 mg per item: Ideal for capsules, not ideal for brownies or cookies.

- Cannot look like a food item.

- Must be labeled with ingredients and potency.

6. Capsules

Using ground cannabis and a stable cooking oil, cannabis can be gently heated or browned then allowed to cool. Place a consistent weighed amount in each capsule bottom then cap with a capsule top. This is an excellent way to achieve the same effects as baked goods without any food ingredients.

Gel caps come in regular and vegetarian options as well as a rainbow of colors. Capsules can be bought at most pharmacies, health food stores, and even on Amazon.

Always include ingredients and dosing information on any products. Always follow labeling requirements in your area including ingredients list, dosing information, and expiration date if applicable. Creating a website with thorough information on each product is always a good idea.

8

Retail: Vapor Lounges; Hemp, Hydroponics, and Online-Only Stores; Compassion Clubs and Dispensaries

Another opportunity in the cannabis space is retail operations. Retail stores such as vapor lounges, and hemp and hydroponics stores, tend to have lower legal risks with low- to mid-level return. They tend to do better in underserviced areas where they are far from other vapor lounges and hemp stores or hydroponic stores.

As online businesses grow, storefront numbers are shrinking. Online businesses are more easily able to pass savings along as they do not require expensive retail space to succeed. Smokazon.com is a good example of an online-only store.

Despite the growth of the online industry, there will always be a place for storefronts and face-to-face services. The following sections include a few examples of retail services you might consider. For a more in-depth look at starting a business, see *Start & Run a Marijuana Dispensary or Pot Shop*, also published by Self-Counsel Press.

1. Vapor Lounges

Vapor lounges are the new pubs. They offer a friendly space for people of legal age to consume cannabis with friends and like-minded people in a social environment. Think of them as the equivalent of "bring your own wine" restaurants. As of the writing of this book, vapor lounges do not sell any cannabis legally in Canada. Some US states allow for vapor lounges and fewer still have lounges that are licensed to dispense.

Vapor lounges are a great way of developing culture, marketing a brand, and creating community. They tend to do well in urban areas or areas with large postsecondary student populations.

The basic rules for vapor lounges for guests are: "Don't sell, don't buy, don't mooch, and don't come here drunk." You must be strict about these rules otherwise violators will undo all your hard work and turn a festive oasis of positivity into a boring truck stop lounge of despair.

Drunk crowds are very different than high crowds — ask any comedian. Alcohol and cannabis produce different cultural vibrations. Any music or comedy shows, or other performances, or programming you add to the mix should be done with this in mind. It has been my experience that it is a good idea to avoid mixing alcohol and cannabis — it will increase the effects of the alcohol, and all its related issues. Moderate to heavy drunkenness mixed with cannabis can be a volatile mix that can lead to physical altercations associated with being drunk and rowdy. Also, very drunk people are more likely to throw up if they consume cannabis on top of their alcohol.

Comedy nights, live music, or DJs go very well together with cannabis culture and they also support the local talent pool.

Vapor lounges tend to target the 18 to 35 crowd and tourists. Local oldtimers will come out on occasion, or if it's worth their while, or for special events. You can also cater to sports fans, poker fans, women, students, ethnicities, DJs/musicians, science geeks, gamers, etc. Know your crowd and what brings many of them, and their friends, in to have an enjoyable experience.

If you want to have a comedy night at your vapor lounge but don't know where to start, contact a comedy night organizer at one of the vapor lounges in Vancouver, Toronto, Los Angeles, Portland, or Seattle. They may be more than happy to tell you how to organize an open mic comedy night. Depending on where you are, they may be able to put you in touch with one or more comics, or comedy show organizers, local to your area.

While lounges are important culture-building enterprises, they have limited ability for revenue streams without cannabis sales. They offer a pub-like experience but do not sell cannabis in this case. They are limited to retail items such as pipes, bongs, papers, juice, soda, prepackaged snacks, internet and gaming stations, etc. They usually sell, rent, and provide vaporizers and/or bongs as an added revenue stream. I have seen some lounges that will store your bong there and let no one use it except you. This is much like a diner mug with your name on it and adds a nice personal touch for your regulars.

Vapor lounges are commercial operations and therefore open to the public. This means that many processes required to open any commercial business fall under the jurisdiction of its local municipality. Zoning, food production, seating capacity, bathrooms, fire exits, and more will all have to be addressed before opening. Consult a lawyer who is familiar with local municipal codes. You can also speak with your elected municipal representative, but be wary of the prohibition mindset.

Because of limited revenues, some lounges charge a door fee for one-time visits or special events; some vapor lounges also charge a minimum seating fee, some charge membership fees (the longer your membership commitment, the cheaper the fee, for example: $5 per day, $15 per week, $40 per month). As selling cannabis or alcohol is not an option, you must be creative with your business plan and produce as many multiple successful revenue streams as possible.

Follow the Amsterdam coffeeshop model for staffing: hire smart, young, friendly students to run your frontline. Offer clean, high-quality working bongs and vaporizers that can be hygienically shared. This means all house bongs must be thoroughly cleaned before every use; all house vaporizers and mouthpieces must also be hygienically cleaned and scrubbed in a sink with soap and hot water before every use. A vase brush is a useful tool. I have also seen magnetic brushes that scrub the inside of bongs by moving a magnet on the outside of the glass. Here is a link to a video to make your own: www.youtube.com/watch?v=Gs3ZDUUSTFE. There are also off-the-shelf products that exist. It is a nice touch to offer ice cubes and steel screen (not brass) free of charge upon request.

Currently, Canadian municipalities can regulate tobacco consumption with existing bylaws. Cities cannot however, regulate the consumption of cannabis as it is federally regulated, although some do try. As each province falls in line with the federal *Cannabis Act* they will likely update their provincial legislation in regards to tobacco, impaired driving, zoning, and adult use of cannabis. This new legislation will empower municipalities to decide where cannabis can or cannot be consumed or possessed, regulate impaired driving limits, and support municipalities with legislation and proper zoning guidelines. It is important to note that medical cannabis use and consumption is federally regulated and could exclude licensed medical users from some provincial restrictions. (See Chapter 26, section 1. on becoming a medical user in Canada.)

In Canada, it is legal to provide a space for people to consume cannabis providing it is in compliance with zoning. Explaining the maximum amounts to first-time patrons is considerate and good business; this is also good time to encourage people to get their medical licenses if they want to possess larger amounts of cannabis than 30 g and grow more than four plants. The provinces regulate where it can be consumed under the *Cannabis Act*, but not under any current tobacco-related laws or bylaws.

In the US, if legal, each state will outline the rules for consumption whether in public or lounges.

Consider creating a concise handbill explaining the rules to tourists in your area. See section 5. in Chapter 20, about advertising, for a sample.

Vapor lounges are open to the public so be prepared to kick out the occasional customer who resells cannabis within your establishment. Also expect the occasional visit from local police or state/provincial inspectors — uniformed and plainclothed. Patrons caught reselling or with excessive amounts of cannabis without a license could be investigated, detained, and charged.

Approximate Start-up Costs for a Vapor Lounge

Basic vapor lounge start-up costs (without a food license)

First two + last two months of rent + hydro + internet

Rolling papers, grinders, pipes, and bongs	$10,000
Snack food inventory	$2,000
Retail pipes and bongs	$3,000
Audio, video, WiFi equipment	$5,000
Display cabinets and shelving	$3,000
Tables, chairs, fridge, basic decor	$5,000
Bongs and vaporizers	$2,000
Initial staffing costs	$2,000
Security system	$1,000

Does not include marketing, external signage, costs of licensing, and incorporation.

Start-up costs are variable and can be as low as $30,000 to $40,000, as a conservative, educated guess.

1.1 Come-down products

If you're going to be running a lounge, you should know about come-down products. There are several new products on the market for people who eat too much edibles — those who "cookied out" or "greened out." The term probably comes from "passed out" in reference to consuming too much alcohol.

If you have ever seen someone eat too much cannabis, he or she was likely very intoxicated and possibly unable to stay awake.

While debilitating, it won't cause physical damage nor can it kill you if you ingest too much cannabis. However, people with histories of mental illness should not consume cannabis without medical supervision.

There are several branded products on the market that hasten the metabolizing process. One product called UNDOO claims to be an "all-natural emergency supplement intended to ease the effects of cannabis over consumption." Products like this should be made available in all locations where cannabis is sold and as an over-the-counter product at pharmacies.

Don't do what some Toronto Police officers did: They raided a dispensary then illegally took several edibles. They ate a single edible and waited impatiently. They didn't feel anything so they ate one or two more edibles. They were brought to the hospital and were "hallucinating" before being sent home and suspended with pay. ("Toronto police who allegedly ate pot edibles on duty called for help after 'hallucinations'",) *CBC News*, January 29, 2018, www.cbc.ca/news/canada/toronto/two-toronto-police-officers-suspended-pot-hallucinating-marijuana-cannabis-1.4509048).

2. Hemp Stores

Hemp stores are retail storefronts for cannabis-related accessories, clothing, and other retail items. They are lower legal risk start-ups yielding, in my professional opinion, a possible 10 to 20 percent increase in profits year over year much like any non-cannabis retail storefront. Many items are easily obtained through a small number of wholesale suppliers in Canada. The US has many options depending on your region. They can be trendy gathering places and excellent places for tourists and visitors, or small retail-only locations. Hemp stores can specialize in some of these areas for added marketability: glass, glass making, clothing, books, memorabilia, posters, or even T-shirts.

When you start thinking of what kind of merchandise to offer, in Canada, hbicanada.com, westcoastgifts.ca, and bobhq.com, are good places to start. You will need to supply a credit check and all orders are COD unless otherwise negotiated. In the US there are dozens of suppliers in each area, that can be found using a search engine.

It is important to note that hemp stores selling hydroponic equipment are usually frowned upon by Canadian law enforcement; however, this could change under the *Cannabis Act* and legalization in general. Legality of seed selling is not yet clear under the Act.

If you are looking for inspiration and are in Barrie, Ontario, please take the time to visit www.liquidchrome.ca; they specialize in glass art and many pieces there could be considered museum grade. Some pipes or glass art will sell for more than $20,000. This is fantastic example of a hemp store that specializes in one aspect of the industry and will draw the public in — not just cannabis enthusiasts — by a clear understanding and sheer passion for glass art, and then capitalize on it. I would consider them a hemp store but with an excellent marketing strategy.

Each US state will, at the moment, have its own laws. Federally it is illegal to possess viable cannabis seeds. (Refer to Chapter 4 for more about seeds.)

3. Hydroponics Stores

Hydroponics stores tend to attract smaller craft growers. Hydroponic equipment can be ordered online and therefore it can be difficult to compete if you are running a brick and mortar retail hydroponics store.

Most hydroponic suppliers will usually require you to have a physical storefront before securing a supply contract. Online-only stores will be a hard sell to most suppliers. There are an endless number of online suppliers making it difficult to compete, including Amazon and eBay.

I would not recommend a hydroponics-only store as a stand-alone investment. It could work with other related projects such as an established retail hemp/bong store or craft producer. I have seen tattoo shops and gardening shops that sell hydroponic equipment as a side product, for example. Only under these conditions would it be strategically and financially advantageous to have a retail store as it would also gain easy access to wholesale prices and new products.

One of the many ways hydroponics stores increase revenues is by buying their products in bulk and repackaging them for retail. Sometimes products can be white labeled, which is a good branding opportunity. Nutrients and additives are primary selling products as well as products such as growing media and electrical equipment.

Stores can also obtain used hydroponic equipment available through sites such as Craigslist, Kijiji, or auction sites. Although sold as is, excellent deals can be found, sometimes lower than wholesale. Be prepared to have space and tools for salvaging parts in order to assemble fully functioning units.

Being able to locate a specific piece of new and reliable hydroponic equipment quickly and easily is not always straightforward, especially when urgent matters arise. Being "that" store could have many rewards, especially if craft producers would be permitted to sell their products to the public legally and easily.

It is not clear how favorable law enforcement will be with hydroponic stores that sell cannabis seeds and paraphernalia in one location, in both Canada and the US. High Intensity Discharge (HID) lights are sold for near cost at most commercial electrical suppliers and they are also a good source for wiring supplies, fluorescent lighting, lighting fixtures, and stands.

Inventory start-up costs for this kind of business can be as low as $30,000, in my estimate.

4. Online-Only Stores

It is possible to create a successful online-only store by starting small with popular legal retail items such as hydroponic equipment, cannabis accessories, hemp, or branded clothing.

Some states do not allow interstate commerce for cannabis-related items. Consult a lawyer to know which states and/or countries you can and cannot ship to. Be especially aware of any laws surrounding shipping across state or international lines.

There are many online marketing opportunities such as affiliate programs whereby visitors would order via your website, or a redirected website, and the go-between gets an affiliate commission on a sale. This strategy works well if you have strong supporting social media with good community engagement. See sites smokazon.com and everyonedoesit.com; they grow a little bit every year. I have also seen accessories listed on etsy.com for sale, but no content related to cannabis (likely because of the fact that cannabis is illegal federally in the US).

If you have a storefront, you should also have a supporting website with a shopping cart. People search for shops online even if they plan to visit a retail location in person. Consider blogging as well (see Chapter 20 for more on this).

If you visit Chris Ramsay (magician) or Peter McKinnon (photographer and videographer) on YouTube, you will see that they produce simple but high-end, well-lit, good audio, well edited, regular, personable content. They do 12 to 15 YouTube shows (or webisodes) per month. Plus they strongly cross-promote on Facebook, Twitter, and Instagram. They have experienced substantial growth in popularity, especially lately. All their early videos are available and worth studying from the point of view of growing social media viewerships and turning it into a self-sustaining work.

If you look at YouTube account customgrow420, you may notice that he started off with video content of him consuming cannabis in different and funny ways — he still does. His original goal was to hit 100,000 YouTube subscribers.

He produces four to six videos each month sometimes promoting specific products or brands. He now has more than 1 million subscribers and probably travels and earns a living from his blogging revenues. There are many examples of people charting their own paths online.

Proper use of hashtags is critical in social media and blogging. Second to that is interesting use of emojis and GIFs. Spend time learning about how best to use these features.

Avoid blogging about breakups, arguments, or business disputes. Putting other people down, personal drama, rants, and anything negative should not be broadcast. Use positivity only whenever possible.

At some point you will want to research search engine marketing and organic search results, especially when it comes to Google, the major search engine. There are people you can hire to look after your online ads if you don't have time to take care of the myriad details, but it is something you really should learn about yourself before handing the reins to another.

See Chapter 20 for more about marketing your online business.

5. Compassion Clubs and Dispensaries

Compassion clubs or cannabis dispensaries are interchangeable names, but they come in two kinds: medical and adult/recreational use. If you are required to submit a medical document as part of the service or membership, then it is a medical organization. Some medical clubs are strict and require original physician's documents that are verified before accessing services. Some will accept cards from any (even a competitor's) dispensary.

A valid medical document needs to contain the the patient's name, date of birth, a clear diagnosis, and ideally, related symptoms for accessing cannabis. By definition, it must be signed by a practicing physician in good standing with his or her state or provincial medical college.

Sometimes recreational clubs, also called dispensaries, are member-based (where you submit your ID and fill out a membership form) and others offer walk-in service, some without any sign-up process at all.

There is no straightforward application process to legally set up a dispensary except in very few municipalities. In most circumstances, setting up a dispensary is considered illegal or has fallen within the gray area of the law.

It is probably illegal to set up a dispensary without any application process. Even if your municipality has a zoning policy for dispensaries there is an almost guarantee that law enforcement and health inspectors will show up and check you out, and possibly raid you.

To own or run or have a part in an unlicensed dispensary is to be a bit of rogue. Depending on where your dispensary is located, it could result in quick police action. Motivation is key if you want to run a gray market dispensary.

Medical dispensaries play an important role in the legalization of cannabis and medical cannabis. They challenge the laws in important ways that, in the past, have led to positive changes in cannabis reform.

Dispensaries are storefronts for the distribution of medical cannabis. They can be slow to build a client base and not straightforward to market successfully, but are not expensive by corporate standards. It has been my experience that for the first 500 members, you can expect 1 to 6 percent (5 to 30 member visits) of the membership to purchase on each business day under ideal conditions.

Elements that affect sales at a dispensary can include quality, price, varieties, reputation, staff service, ease of access, proximity to other cannabis retailers, website, social media, weather, long weekends, time of month, time of year, and neighborhood issues.

Marketing is a huge consideration when you're running a retail space, and it may take many months or years to mature. See Chapter 20 on marketing and branding for things to consider.

In my opinion, it is not a good idea to open a dispensary in Canada, especially as a stand-alone business, primarily because of its legal status in the months leading up to legalization. There are a small number of municipalities that are open to dispensaries but it could still be difficult to navigate before laws are formalized.

9
Importing and Exporting

The import and export of cannabis is not allowed at the federal level in the US or by way of the US, meaning all cannabis that is legal at state levels has to be sourced and grown in that state. There is no transporting across international borders allowed.

Health Canada's Licensed Producers (LPs) can obtain permission to import and export cannabis to and from Canada. This is a unique opportunity despite the fact that international agreements limit most foreign governments' abilities to produce cannabis. Only a small but growing number of countries allow corporations to produce cannabis or a cannabis product, in high enough quality and quantity, and have a foreign government that allows for the export of dried cannabis into and from Canada.

There are a small number of countries that actively export cannabis in large part despite international agreements but also because until recently, there has not been a market for selling cannabis legally and internationally — until now. Consult with or hire an international lawyer or specialist to start or maintain your import/export affairs, especially if you are new to this type of business and plan on investing substantial resources. The prohibitionist mindset may on occasion impede bureaucratic progress as well so this task could take some perseverance.

It is worth noting that Health Canada has not authorized an import/export-only LP license at the time of writing.

If you wish to import to Canada, you must first find a foreign company or entity (that legally produces dried cannabis). That company must convince its federal government to export it to Canada if it's not already allowed. Approaching the foreign government directly may yield interesting results. Understanding the hierarchy of foreign governments is critical. Some countries will give authority over cannabis to the federal Health Ministry, law enforcement, or the military. Expect overlap with all three.

Currently, the only countries that have corporate or private production of cannabis are Netherlands, Israel, Germany, Costa Rica, Uruguay, and Czech Republic. Other countries are coming on board slowly but surely.

If cannabis and cannabis products can be produced, shipped, and imported into Canada for less money than it costs to produce domestically, you have a promising revenue stream and an advantage over other LPs. Excise taxes will vary from country to country and require a complicated formula. Consult the Canada Border Services Agency (CBSA) for details, as well as an import-export specialist (https://www.cbsa-asfc.gc.ca).

You must make a separate import application for each foreign supplier and a separate export application for each foreign receiver. Your applications will require the following information:

- LP's name, address, and LP number

- Description of the cannabis to be imported

- Quantity to be imported

- THC and CBD percentages

- Supplier's brand name, if applicable

- Name and address of the foreign supplier

- Port of entry

- Address of the CBSA office, sufferance or bonded warehouse receiving the cannabis

- Each mode of transportation used, the country of export, and any country of transit or trans-shipment, if applicable

This information must accompany all deliveries.

Once imported cannabis arrives in Canada, expect it to be domestically retested. It is advisable to do a thorough analysis before exporting bulk quantities to Canada as costly mistakes can happen if the domestic analytic results are not acceptable.

Health Canada import or export licenses for a specific product or order expires 180 days from the date of issue, as of this writing.

10
Outdoor Growing and Greenhouses

In Canada, assuming you are following the rules, Health Canada does not allow for outdoor commercial cannabis growing. You can grow in a greenhouse provided that the greenhouse complies with several security requirements, least of which is that the greenhouse walls are made of concrete or equivalent and sit on a concrete foundation; access must be secured. The numerous hurdles in place make a hobby greenhouse non-licensable by a mom-and-pop operation and better suited for a mid-size or large corporation with an existing LP license.

As a Licensed Producer, you could make an importation application for outdoor, greenhouse-grown, and indoor cannabis through legal import channels. See Chapter 9: Importing and Exporting.

In the US, some states allow for personal outdoor plants. Some states do license outdoor production which is ideal in some environments and will lower the cost of the production, since greenhouses don't need to be built, and these savings can hopefully be passed on to the consumer. Large-scale production licenses are hard to come by and are usually limited in availability. Each state that adopts legalization presents these and other new opportunities.

Economically speaking, it is in the best interest of each state to consume the cannabis produced in that state. There is no legal interstate commerce for cannabis as of yet.

Part 2
Business Considerations Specific to the Cannabis Industry

The cannabis industry might have a lot in common with other industries, but there are also considerations specific to this growing and still, in some ways, wild west industry. Based on my experiences, Part 2 discusses what you should consider as you embark on your venture.

11

Finance: Taxes, Banks, Credit Cards, Payment Services

This chapter takes a look at finances when your business is in cannabis.

1. Taxes

Consult with a lawyer and an accountant in your area to develop a proper tax and banking strategy.

In Canada, cannabis is currently sales tax applicable both federally and provincially plus there is an excise tax. Some provinces do not have harmonized sales tax (HST). Expect to pay collected sales taxes quarterly especially if sales exceed $5,000 per month (generally). Your first $30,000 of business is GST/HST free; after that you need to register for a GST/HST number and start charging and paying those taxes. Ensure your accountant and lawyer have read the legal opinion of tax lawyer David M. Sherman on sales tax and medical cannabis (see camcd-acdcm.ca/wp-content/uploads/2014/06/Does-GST-apply-to-medical-marijuana-June-2014.pdf).

In the US, although cannabis is not legal federally, you may have to deal with state taxation and tax stamps. Consult with tax and legal professionals in your area to be sure you are adhering to local laws as these can vary significantly.

2. Banks, Credit Cards, Payment Services

As a new legal Licensed Producer or other business, you should be able to conduct business like any other legitimate Canadian corporation. This means basic banking, merchant accounts, checks, electronic transfers, etc., should all be available to you once everything is legalized. At first, you can expect some resistance as Canadian financial institutions adjust to their new reality when cannabis is legalized. Some credit unions and similar institutions could be more flexible ("Where Pot Entrepreneurs Go When the Banks Just Say No," *The New York Times Magazine*, January 4, 2018).

Avoid institutions that are US-owned, or do substantial business in the US as the state of their federal law often means your funds would be considered illegally obtained.

Mastercard, Visa, PayPal, and similar large financial brands will likely have policies prohibiting the sale of cannabis, cannabis products or services, or narcotics in the user agreements, even where legal. If they do not have this policy, they probably have a separate policy that specifies they may terminate services because they want to, with no explanation needed or given. You will unlikely be able to extract funds from a terminated account, so beware before you open one. Because many of these companies are publicly traded and operate in the US they must adhere to Securities and Exchange Commission (SEC) rules on money, and federally marijuana/cannabis is still illegal.

If you operate a cannabis business in the US, expect a cash-only business and all the issues that this entails including figuring out where to store your cash if not at a bank. (Will you need a safe? What about security?)

12
Intellectual Property

Intellectual Property (IP) is critical to the cannabis industry because it holds such enormous financial potential. Your imagination is limited to developing a patentable medical product, or a patentable medical delivery device. Developing either of these IP projects could yield a substantial revenue stream for years and years. IP is expensive to establish and it is expensive to do proper research. Each patent must be registered in each country in which you want to hold it. The patent holder must also incur the cost of policing and enforcing the patent. Expect to spend at least $1 million on each IP product or device over the course of two to ten years. The costs are related to legal and approval costs, development, and marketing and distribution.

IP is similar to other financial assets whereby shares can be issued to contributing participants or sold outright. If you think you have an idea that cannot be patented, then it is a trade secret or something you have figured out on your own that may or may not have a returnable value. If your idea can be (easily) duplicated in China or India or elsewhere, you should consider a cost-benefit analysis of such an endeavor.

You will need to consult with a lawyer who specializes in IP in your area to confidentially discuss any opportunities or ideas you may have.

Intellectual property can also be in the form of trademarks. If you develop a brand, you should trademark it, similar to any restaurant trademark. A worst-case scenario would be a competitor taking your design and content, then trademarking it themselves forcing you to rebrand, redesign, and trademark properly anew. See Chapter 20: Marketing and Branding.

13
Insurance and Licenses

1. Insurance

Getting adequate insurance coverage will be tricky in the early days of the ACMPR (Health Canada's Access to Cannabis for Medical Purposes Regulations). Although other pharmaceutical companies and narcotics producers can be insured, insuring licensed producers, and cannabis businesses, tends to scare off some insurers.

Canadian insurance companies that provide specialized coverage for Licensed Producers — and micro-producers — are a matter of time. Initial searching will be inevitable but there are insurance providers under the ACMPR. See Questionnaire 1.

Consult with your lawyer when you do receive an offer for any insurance product. Make sure it addresses all your business needs.

Insurance may not be required with your business; its necessity increases with the size of your business. If you have any financing

Questionnaire 1
Insurance

Shop around for insurance. Consult with your lawyer when you receive an offer for any insurance product. Make sure it addresses all your business needs.

Some critical questions include:

- What happens in case of theft or fire? Property damage? Recall? Adverse reaction?
- What is the process of filing a claim for cannabis that is stolen or lost in a fire?
- Does the insurance cover rebuilding and lost revenue?
- What is the deductible; what is covered and what is not?
- Does the insurance policy cover the Board of Directors and its Operators?

in place, the financier will likely require that you have adequate coverage; you will also want to ensure you are covered in case of theft, fire, etc.

If cannabis is being grown on the property you are insuring, your insurer needs to know. If it is illegal in your area, the insurer might consider you uninsurable.

If you have a background in offering insurance products and services, this large and new industry presents obvious opportunities for the right insurance broker or brokers.

2. Licenses

When running a legal business, there are likely going to be different licenses you need to obtain. These can depend on the area in which you are doing business.

Will you need a city business license? Will you need the paperwork to be a Licensed Producer from Health Canada? Are there different licenses in your area if you're going to be preparing edibles? There are too many variables to list each one in this book, so you will have to do some research in your locality, and speak to local officials, and especially to your accountant and lawyer.

Applications for licenses can include background checks, especially in the cannabis industry. Each member of your team should be prepared for this.

14.
Getting an Audit, an Inspection, or a Recall

You must be audit-ready and inspection-ready at all times when it comes to legal cannabis.

In Canada, under the new rules, your Quality Assurance (QA) person or team will have established written protocols for these eventualities as part of the license application process. The Senior Person In Charge (SPIC) or Responsible Person In Charge (RPIC) will get a call, fax, email, or letter from an auditor indicating he or she will be audited or inspected. Call Health Canada right away and confirm the auditor's name, job title, and contact information. Then have your Person In Charge call the auditor or inspector and sort out issues and meeting details. Try to obtain as much information as possible during that first conversation. Be courteous, friendly, and cooperative. Always be punctual and on time.

Make sure all conversations are followed up by an email to the auditor or inspector summarizing the details so that everything is in writing.

Some questions to ask before an audit or inspection so there are no surprises:

- What is the name of the inspector, and job title?
- What is the name of his or her supervisor, and job title?
- What documents or reports does he or she require as part of the visit?
- How much time does the auditor anticipate requiring?
- What is the scope of inspection — fire, safety, sanitation, security, QA, compliance?
- Is the inspector coming alone? If not, obtain the name and job title of every person coming.

It is normal to schedule an inspection within one to two weeks from notification.

When you speak with an auditor, expect the person to be co-operative but inquisitive. The current strategy for tax auditors is to ask for targeted information — also known as a mini-audit. The person may want you to produce very specific information on a strain, a medical user, a day, a batch, a lot, an analyst, or another LP. If this mini-audit is completed and verified to the auditor's satisfaction, expect nothing or perhaps one more mini-audit. Make sure you receive documentation from the auditor that the audit has been satisfactorily completed every time one happens.

Audits do not always require a physical visit by the auditor. They are usually fully documented by email or fax. Never send data files to an auditor; always send reports in the form of PDFs.

Inspections are not enforcement investigations. Audits are a regulatory requirement and everyone should behave accordingly. Because inspections are a civil matter (not criminal), businesses have a little leeway in determining the time and date of the inspection, which takes place during normal business hours.

If there is a criminal investigation, then your right to remain silent applies. Do not submit any documents without your lawyer's instruction.

Consult your lawyer for a greater understanding of any event of which you are unsure. Instruct the lawyer to ensure all audits and inspections are civil, not criminal.

If cannabis you produced was used in a crime (by no fault of your own), you may be contacted by police or an inspector to supply necessary documents or audit reports. The same will apply to any recalls. You may or may not be informed of the reason for the audit.

Try to see the auditor/inspector as someone trying to maintain a safe and high-quality standard of medicine, and not someone trying to catch you or target you negatively. Enforcement should not be a direct part of the inspector's or auditor's job.

If your product ever experiences a recall, it will be a serious test of your audit-ready skills. Review the sections of the applicable laws with your entire team so you can avoid the time, cost, and aggravation of a recall.

15
Drug Identification Numbers/ National Drug Code

Drug Identification Numbers (DINs) are eight-digit numbers assigned by Health Canada to a drug product prior to the drug being marketed in Canada. It is a way to show that a product has withstood the rigors of safety and medical testing according to Health Canada and it is safe to be marketed and sold.

At the time the ACMPR was published, there were no DINs for cannabis as plant medicine, and this is one reason health claims cannot be made. The process to apply for these in Canada is long and expensive and better suited for Big Cannabis than well-meaning activist or craft producers.

Once one or more DINs are available for cannabis or whole-cannabis products, provincial healthcare plans should start to get involved, thus lowering the cost to the medical user.

Provincial involvement will have an enormous effect on the industry, if or when DINs come into existence. Although years away, it will most likely have a negative effect on smaller LPs.

Each province is ultimately better suited to regulate cannabis production than the federal government, similar to provincial brewery regulations. That is a future evolution of the industry and the ACMPR has helped to kickstart this process. Lobbying your provincial MP or health minister, or state health department representative is a good way to contribute as a responsible corporate entity. There are other intrinsic advantages to meeting and knowing your elected representatives.

Once your product has a DIN, you may have the enormous opportunity to bring that product to foreign markets. Some countries have compatible or comparable standards with Health Canada on natural medicines. Less developed countries have standards lower than Health Canada's drug approval process.

It is probably easier to obtain a DIN in Canada than a National Drug Code number in the US, especially if you are employing cannabis products or cannabinoids. In the US, the National Drug Code is a unique ten-digit, three-segment numeric identifier assigned to each drug listed under Section 510 of the Food, Drug, and Cosmetic Act. The segments identify the labeler or vendor, product (within the scope of the labeler), and trade package (of this product). Since cannabis (legally, called marijuana in the US) is illegal federally in the US, the US Food and Drug Administration (FDA) and Drug Enforcement Agency (DEA) will likely oppose your efforts vigorously.

16
Growing Your Own and Strain/Symptom Correlation

It has been known for years that certain strains are better suited to target specific medical symptoms. A general rule of thumb: Indicas tend to target symptoms below the neck, sativas tend to target symptoms above the neck. Hybridization of cannabis, however, has muddied this rule. Analysis and cannabinoid profiling will assist in determining the correlation. It is the responsibility of pioneers of this new industry to contribute to the growing body of knowledge. This may also be an opportunity to create some intellectual property, in some capacity.

If you are considering whether to be a grower, complete Questionnaire 2 (also available on the download kit).

If you decide to grow yourself, I would recommend no less than a space for 4 HPS bulbs which is 8 ft. x 8 ft. This does not include space for your electrical or watering needs. Anything less

Questionnaire 2
Should You Grow Your Own?

Section A: Infrastructure

- Do you dream of growing your own high-quality cannabis?
- Do you have experience growing your own cannabis? Troubleshooting plant issues?
- Do you have basic carpentry experience for building a grow room?
- Do you have basic electrical understanding for building a grow room?
- Does your electrical panel have spare room for 30 amps to 40 amps?
- Are you OK with the constant slight or heavy smell of cannabis?
- Do you travel rarely or are you rarely away from home for more than 24 hours?

Section B: Lifestyle

- Do you consume 4 g or more per day?
- Do you have 7 to 30 hours per week to devote to your plants? more time is devoted during the harvest and clean up.
- Do you have a spare room with window to use? (for indoor growing)
- Do you have $5,000 to $7,500 in start-up costs plus $4,000 to $7,000 per year in electricity fees (costs comparable between Canada and the US)
- Do you live with few guests and visitors?
- Do you know who your neighbors are? Do you have enough privacy?
- Do you have a disciplined lifestyle for constant and regular plant maintenance
- Do you have a security conscious approach to cannabis production; are you a private person?
- Do you have a hygienic approach to life? Is your personal and workspace clean and orderly?

If you answered yes to most of Section A and answered yes to ALL of Section B, then you might want to consider growing your own indoor cannabis, where legal.

---

may not be worth the financial benefits; it may subsidize your annual consumption, and some people have a real talent for growing and have the ability to produce high-quality, high-yield crops.

Your single largest ongoing cost will be electricity. For each 1,000 watt bulb @ 10 cents per kWh x 12 hours per day x 30 days per month = about $40 + taxes per month per bulb.

If you had a six-light grow room, your other key electrical devices would be:

- Air conditioner x 1

- Oscillating fans x 4

- Exhaust fan x 1

- Pumps, timers, and meters

It is easily possible that your monthly electric bill could be $300 to $400 per month ($3,600 to $4,800 per year in Canada or the US). LED lights are a promising new technology which reduces your heat and electrical costs while increasing yields. There are 4 ft. x 8 ft. LED arrays in the $1,600 per unit range. One company called Fluence seems to be taking the lead in this field (http://fluence.science). Using LEDs will drive up your start-up costs but it could reduce your electrical and air conditioning requirements while potentially increasing the quality of your cannabis.

Growing at home or full time is really a lifestyle choice of almost constant, daily plant care. You have to be security and hygiene conscious at all times and execute a daily and weekly list of responsibilities.

Even if you live in a place where it has been legalized, cannabis is still valued highly enough that criminals will try to steal it or worse.

In Canada, the ACMPR allows for individual medical users to grow their own or designate a producer. A designated producer can only grow for two patients. Only four caregivers can occupy a single address. The reason to grow your own is really one of lifestyle and cost savings. If you consume 3 g of cannabis per day and your cost of retail is $8/g then 4 g x $ 8 x 365 = $11,680 per year. The cost of setting up a grow room in a bedroom is $5,000 to $8,000.

Growing tip: Cannabis expresses purple hues when the temperature drops to 5°C to 8°C for six hours before the lights come on.

If cannabis is being grown on your property, you should inform your insurance provider. Have a backup insurer in mind first in case there are any issues and your insurer decides it will not insure anything to do with cannabis. See Chapter 13 for more about insurance.

1. Cost of Production

As a grower of cannabis for public consumption, your cost of producing high-quality, dried cannabis should be between $2.50–$4.00 per gram, a half kilogram for every 1,000-watt HPS lightbulb. While this does take into account staffing, location, utilities, and overhead, it does not take into account high-level security, analyses, regulatory compliance, and marketing costs.

If a plant requires 10 to 15 weeks of flowering (as is the case with sativa), a higher cost to produce is created and likely, this higher cost is passed on to the consumer. Determining your cost per square meter, per week, and per month is very useful information.

Rule of thumb: As a craft grower, $1 of retail price reflects one week in a flower room. So, a $10 retail gram should take ten weeks to flower, vegetative time not included.

2. You Can Always Be a Canadian Licensed Producer (or US Equivalent) That Does Not Grow

At the time of writing, Health Canada regulations allow for licensed producers to buy, sell, transport, and destroy cannabis amongst themselves as well as import or export cannabis. Producer prices, wholesale prices, and retail prices have established themselves early and continue to evolve as the market matures in size and legitimacy. Becoming an LP will allow you to do business with other LPs, acting as a go-between for several large or small LPs and a distribution network. Be wary, however, as too many go-between transactions can increase the cost of a product above competitive prices.

If you are unable to obtain an LP license from Health Canada for security reasons, you cannot be a corporate director nor an officer, but you can be staff and/or a shareholder. You can also subcontract to another LP but you would need to comply with their internal LP operating procedures also called Standard Operating Procedures (SOPs).

Pooling resources with other producers could be a delicate but important matter to broach. Written agreements create clear expectations for all parties, and their compensation. Avoid verbal agreements especially for large, long-term projects (get everything in writing). Written agreements are more important than ever because, when done properly, they can be enforced by the court system. This applies to agreements between businesses, as well as agreements within your own business.

3. Growing and Wholesaling versus Growing and Retailing

Many growers and other interested parties will have a tendency to want to grow as well as retail their product themselves as part of their business plan. There is absolutely nothing wrong with wanting to maximize available business by doing more than one thing, but be aware of the amount of work you would be taking on if you choose to not specialize in one niche, but rather grow and retail your product too.

A closer look at what is required to apply for a Canadian LP license reveals an enormous amount of preparation on QA and record-keeping. The amount of record-keeping for plant production is daunting, and the amount of record-keeping for retailing to customers is equally daunting. Doing both well will require the highly specialized skills of a few well-paid experts in the pharmaceutical and drug manufacturing world. If you are considering this robust full-service approach, I would recommend that you phase in distribution at least 6 to 12 months after you are in operation. If you are serious about providing comprehensive services, you may consider two or three separate LP applications for production, distribution, and analysis.

Your greatest challenge once you receive your LP is to maintain your license. LPs are always one or two inspections or audits away from losing their license to operate.

Recovering from a loss of license will be devastating to your ability to continue business.

4. Understanding Federal Secure Storage Levels and Maximum Storage

It is expected as a retailer, distributor, or producer that you will have adequate secure storage for cannabis and its products no matter where you are located.

The basis of Health Canada's Directive On Physical Security Requirements For Controlled Substances is based on a predetermined street value that Health Canada places on all controlled substances. Health Canada uses street value based on the assumption that the substance is stolen and is to be sold in the black market. (https://www.canada.ca/en/health-canada/services/health-concerns/reports-publications/controlled-substances-precursor-chemicals/directive-physical-security-requirements-controlled-substances-licensed-dealers-security-requirements-storage.html, accessed March, 2017)

Although each province may have different security standards, it is likely to be based on Health Canada's Directive. It specifies construction requirements for each increasing level of security which will determine your desired security level and its required elements.

In Canada, you will need to review Health Canada's Directive On Physical Security Requirements For Controlled Substances to determine your desired security level and its required elements.

In the US, each state will dictate security requirements and maximum storage limits.

5. Security-Storage Breakdown

In Canada, the Health Canada Security Directives value all cannabis products at $10,000/kg or $10 per gram based on the assumption that, if it were stolen, this would be its black market value.

There are three variables that determine your security level:

1. Where you are in Canada — proximity to mid-sized or large cities — Region I, II, or III.

2. Which controlled substance is being produced — dried cannabis, in this case.

3. What is your desired maximum storage amount of dried cannabis.

Producing in or near a large city increases the security requirements. Conversely, producing in remote parts of Canada lowers the security requirements.

These directives only apply to two areas — building security and vault security. Level 3 or 4 is possible with off-the-shelf security systems and is fairly straightforward with a small investment budget. A quick read of levels 3, 4, and 5, reveals the methodology of the directives — each successive level adds a new security feature or upgrades a preexisting feature. The security infrastructure requirements successively progresses until level 11.

A quick look at the security-storage breakdown list determines a few realities. For the enthusiastic grower there is a natural tendency to obtain the highest security level; however, a closer look at security level 11 reveals that it is highly cost-prohibitive; and why would you need to actually store more than 15,000 kg of dried cannabis? Or even 3,125 kg or 625 kg? As a small- or mid-level LP you would need to store far less than 15,000 kg especially since you will have rotating inventory. The product should go to market as soon as possible, or better, as soon as it is ready. A 25 kg to 125 kg storage limit should be enough for most craft producers. As a worst-case scenario, you can rent storage space from another licensed entity.

Security for level 6, Region I allows for 25 kgs or 55 lbs of dried cannabis in storage. No limits on plant numbers. This is enough for most LP grow facilities: 50 to 150 1,000 watt lamps with rotating inventory.

Because LPs are no longer limited by plant numbers, production is based on maximizing square footage of growing space — not grams per plant. Smaller plants also produce more consistency and uniformity than large plants which produce high quality at the top and poor quality at the bottom.

Each security level 4 or security level 5 location can store five kilograms of dried cannabis — small enough for a co-op comprised of two to ten people to run and self-supply — perhaps even supply a few more licensed medical users. A co-op this small will likely have to outsource its analysis and Quality Assurance. This would be a successful example of transitioning from the Designated Grower program to micro-producer under the ACMPR, assuming the costs can be covered. You can start small with a level 4 or 5 LP operation but level 6, 7, or 8 security should cover most LPs' needs.

While a co-op model of business is acceptable to most people, the regulatory requirements make it too difficult to realize.

Here is the entire text for the requirements for level 3 security. Even a level 3 LP will be able to buy and sell from other LPs.

- level 3 — 1 kg

- level 4 — 1 kg

- level 5 — 5 kg

- level 6 — 25 kg

- level 7 — 125 kg

- level 8 —- 625 kg

- level 9 — 3,125 kg

- level 10 — 15,000 kg

- level 11 — more than 15,000 kg

* Levels 1, 2, and sometimes 3 are for research and analytic licenses only

The following is a quick Health Canada breakdown for each security level and its maximum storage amount of dried cannabis:

Security level 3 is the lowest possible security level for an LP and applies to Region III (remote regions) only. See Health Canada's document "Physical Security Requirements For Controlled Substances" to review its appendixes to determine your security level.

Security level 4 would have the same storage capacity (1 kg) but for a location closer to a large urban center. The difference in setup costs for level 3 versus level 4 is relatively small.

If you plan to have security level higher than level 7 (125 kg storage), you should consider a cage, instead of a safe, due to space requirements.

Physical security compliance will require several documents detailing each layer and item of security. Expect to submit a Security Report that includes some of these documents:

- Building plans detailing security elements

- A description of the security system design

- List of specific equipment manufacturers and models including images

- Locations for the four security areas and vault or cage

The four security areas are as follows:

1. Uncontrolled licensee areas are a buffer zone which will give a clear indication to the public that ownership and responsibility for behavior in this space rests with the licensee.

2. Controlled licensee areas are all areas of the building to which the general public (delivery personnel, customers, etc.) has access on a restricted basis (specific times of the day or night).

3. Restricted areas are those which should only be accessible to employees with a need for access through general security areas.

4. Secure areas are restricted areas where highly sensitive equipment and information as well as material to which access is restricted to authorized personnel.

The ability to consult in sourcing and installing security systems for other LPs could prove to be a valuable skill (and create a revenue stream).

In the US, as cannabis is illegal federally, there is no comprehensive rule that would cover the whole country. Check with your individual State Department of Health for any required security or storage initiatives.

For more on security see Chapter 23.

6. Education and Certifications for Growers

As cannabis comes into the mainstream the need for education becomes obvious. Education with cannabis comes in two forms — workshops and certifications. You or your staff could attend these for professional development purposes, or you could consider hosting them and selling spaces as an additional revenue stream.

Workshops are short, concise classes intended to familiarize people with various aspects of cannabis production and refinement. They are usually taught by someone knowledgeable but not necessarily an expert. They tend to attract young or cottage industry types.

Workshops tend to be two to ten hours long, usually on the weekend in a casual environment.

Some topics for workshops could include:

- Closet growing

- Clones and mother plants

- Baking cannabis

- Extraction class

- Budtending

- Cannabis-specific business projects

- Food handling (can be a certified class tied to municipal requirements)

All of these topics could have beginner, advanced, and related components. If you decide to hold workshops, start small and gauge how substantial the interest is in learning about small aspects of cannabis production and refinement.

Colorado has several certification requirements for certain jobs within the state. (See thcuniversity.org for details.) Other states are in various stages of development. There are no required certifications for entry-level jobs in Canada.

Certification is inevitable as legalization unfolds. As with the alcohol industry there will be thousands of legal jobs created requiring basic and advanced certifications in handling, retail, and production as time goes on.

Earlier in the book, I offered up this list of possible jobs in the cannabis industry; here it is again as ideas for workshops or certifications in Table 3.

Table 3
Workshops or Certifications

Basic Certifications	Advanced Certifications
Brew technician	Master brewer
Events management	Brew master
Equipment maintenance	Quality assurance
Security	Human resources
Security equipment	Information technology
Compliance	Accounting
Supply management	Insurance provider
Distributors	Legal work (trademark, copyright, labor)
Transportation	
Retail	
Bartender	
Bar manager	
School (teachers to certify individuals)	
Bookkeepers, payroll	
Safety officer (WHMIS)	
Unions/union representatives	
Packaging and labeling	
Marketing, merchandising, and promotions	
Dial-a-bottle type services	

These are but a few of the possible workshops or certifications you could offer or seek.

17
Software and Hardware

It is difficult to imagine any mid-level or larger producer or retailer without an integrated software database. Your software must cover seed to sale; that is, it must record every transaction between producer to medical user, producer to producer, and anytime a batch or lot of cannabis is sown, harvested, dried, packaged, analyzed, stored, sold, transferred, or destroyed, in any location where cannabis is legal.

Your software should integrate these features:

- Customer Management System (CMS) for tracking customer orders past and present

- Point of Sale (POS) software

- Inventory control

- Security and management functionality

- Invoicing: buying/selling

- Customized reporting: reports for audits, and regular financial reports

- Accounting and bookkeeping: reporting, accounts payable and receivable

- Labeling: being able to print customized labels with required information

- Web functionality: update your website, or other online assets

- Social media functionality (optional but good to have)

Whichever software package you decide on, ensure that is audit-ready. Make sure your lawyer, SPIC, RPIC, QA, and your financial officer/accountant, agree on all reporting, accounting, and bookkeeping procedures. Include those procedures in your LP internal manual.

Canadian cannabis users and enthusiasts tend to be more protective of their private information than average Canadians. If you decide to go with cloud computing, ensure that the servers are encrypted at both ends and physically located in Canada. Local software can be more secure than cloud computing if you provide adequate safeguards. You are responsible and accountable for securing the private personal or medical information. Having a confidentiality policy on your website is a good first step.

On the topic of written policies, you should also have a written nondiscrimination policy.

As an LP, you can expect occasional calls from police to confirm the registry of a client. These calls will come at all hours of the day, any time of year. Having a reliable plan to deal with police issues quickly and efficiently 24/7/365 will earn the gratitude of a happy client who will likely tell many people of his or her adventures with the police and how you saved the day on a long weekend near the cottage; as well as the potential respect of reasonable law enforcement who will appreciate that you are not some fly-by-night organization. Expect less organized businesses to respond slowly to these requests.

Any other requests from law enforcement agencies should be in writing and reviewed by your lawyer, whether you are in Canada or the US, especially where personal health information is involved.

Licensed producers can expect occasional requests from clients for "everything I bought in 2017" or "Help, I lost my receipts for the month of January." These requests tend to come around tax filing season. Good software will make these requests simpler to handle.

Most point of sale and customer management systems are tablet compatible, including cash drawer if needed. However, you should know the answer to these questions regardless of which POS/CMS system you use:

- Are you retaining personal or health information? If so, does information storage conform with privacy regulations?

- Is the data you collect stored locally or in the cloud?

- Where are the cloud servers stored? How are they protected and backed up?

I expect that blockchain technology will develop solutions to these issues in the future.

18

Personal Possession and Transporting

In Canada, at the time of writing, the ACMPR allows the medical user to carry no more than 150 grams on your person at any time, even if your 30-day supply may exceed this amount. You can carry up to your annual supply (with you or in your trunk) if you are in transit from your producer to your residence for the purpose of storing it at your residence. Documentation will be required if there is any issue; never waive your rights during a police search or police investigation such as a vehicle or highway traffic stop or during an infraction. Medical users cannot receive more than a 30-day supply, not to exceed 150 grams from any single LP at any one time. Under the Canadian *Cannabis Act*, you are limited to 30 grams of dried cannabis.

In the US, police traffic stops are notorious for rights violations. Some states consider smell probable cause to detain you and search you and your car and its passengers. Always stay under your state's limits and never cross a state line with cannabis without consulting a lawyer and/or knowing the laws in your area.

1. Secure Transport and Courier Services

If you intend to transport or ship cannabis products as a courier, be sure of the laws in your area and of those in the locations to which you are transporting or shipping.

At the time of writing, in Canada, Licensed Producers can provide cannabis via mail order only to their customers. They can also buy and sell cannabis from other LPs in accordance with the ACMPR as well as receive international packages containing cannabis products or genetics. These activities clearly require the use of a courier that may not be up to Canada Post or United States Postal Service standards.

There are several levels or types of couriers. The easiest way to sort them is by the maximum insurable amount to be transported at any one time. You can also sort them by what class of products they are delivering — less than $500, jewelry and currency, narcotics, and pharmaceutical products, dangerous goods, etc.

Using a bonded courier, proper packaging, and labeling is all that Health Canada requires. If you decide to courier product to customers, as the courier company owner you would decide what direction you are going in providing services. Transport does not need to be only about cannabis. Jewelry, bullion, and pharmaceutical drugs are just some of the high-value products that all need to be reliably picked up and delivered. Most LPs will also want secure waste services for the discarded papers and documents as well as sterile waste services. Being competitive in terms of price and service is key.

Low value packages such as business documents or store purchases can double as a secondary mail service, but worthy of pursuit depending on the demographics of your area and proximity to large urban centers. Transporting dangerous goods such as fireworks or weapons could also be promising but it does stray away from the cannabis industry.

Speak to a business insurance sales representative as they will guide you through any certifications needed. You may also need to have your courier vehicle(s) upgraded for security and communication.

If you live near an LP which is 90 minutes away by car, or more, to its closest urban city, then it is almost certain that they will need ongoing courier services if they do not already have an existing relationship or developed one in house. Relying on Canada Post is too slow and FedEx and UPS costs could be substantial.

Having a quick, reliable delivery service is critical to businesses and customers. Branding and marketing, although limited, is key. Owning a delivery company is moderately straightforward in that it only requires adequate insurance (bondability). You will need to know in advance what is the maximum dollar value that your delivery vehicle can carry at any one time.

Depending on the amount, your insurer may require specifics such as a commercial car alarm system, an additional security person, a panic button wired to a live call center, or simply reinforced windows.

19
Flying

Medical users with valid Health Canada licenses are allowed to fly domestically (within Canada) with medical cannabis limited to their 30-day prescription or 150 g, whichever is less. Vaporizer pens for consuming extracts are more airport friendly but check the rules ahead of time to be sure. Always carry some documentation that you are a legal medical cannabis user, including labeled prescription bottles and any license you have. I have a cell phone picture of my medical license issued by Health Canada.

Post legalization, you will be able to possess up to 30 g of dried cannabis, or equivalent, on your person, including domestic flights.

You cannot leave Canada with cannabis in your possession even if it is legal to possess in your country of origin and legal in your destination.

Health Canada states that your medical use and LP licenses are not valid outside Canada in that they are not recognized by any foreign governments. Foreign nongovernment organizations (NGOs), privately owned dispensaries, and some state licensed dispensaries may choose to recognize your license for the purpose of providing your access while out of country.

Do not carry any Health Canada documents with you when you cross the US border from Canada. Your car and clothes should not smell of cannabis in the least because the smell of cannabis can trigger a secondary search, which is a detailed search of everything you are carrying. If border agents discover you are a medical cannabis user — legal or not — you may be barred or refused entry because cannabis, while legal in certain states, is not legal federally in the US at this time. At best you will be detained and thoroughly searched. It is very easy for a border agent to bar you from entry to the US.

Some foreigners have been permanently banned from entry to the US because they admitted to a border guard to smoking cannabis many years ago.

It is also possible that you could be barred from entering the US if you are a foreigner who works for a unionized government-owned distributor or government licensed producer, so if your business is in Canada, be aware of this possibility.

If you are flying within a state (e.g., leaving California and arriving elsewhere within California), you are probably not breaking state law if you are carrying your legal medical marijuana in a properly labeled prescription container; however, airports and air transit are governed at the federal level and you could be violating one or more federal laws. Consult a lawyer before doing so, even for small personal amounts.

If you are considering how to transport wholesale cannabis or other product, refer back to Chapter 18, ensure you read up on the laws in your area and the areas to which and through which you wish to ship product. Consult your lawyer.

20
Marketing and Branding

According to Health Canada, cannabis is a powerful narcotic with no proven therapeutic properties and therefore no medical claims can be attached to it at this time. This description may change as the laws change but I don't anticipate this in the foreseeable future.

In marketing cannabis, you are bound by the same rules that apply to pharmaceutical companies and to federally regulated narcotics. In Canada your product cannot be advertised openly and to the public.

Despite these limitations, if you see almost endless opportunities, it is a mixed blessing. It is great that you understand how many vastly different ways the industry can be tapped, but beware of spreading yourself too thin. There are many specialized skills required to produce and market cannabis. Rare is the person who can do it all and do it well. A well-honed team of individuals with high-caliber business skills is a good solution.

If you are producing dried cannabis, your business plan must include a way to distribute, retail, or sell it to another business or person with the goal of constantly moving inventory. Connecting with other LPs, dispensaries, organizations, and healthcare practitioners requires time and energy. Some LPs will be good at retailing but not good at producing and vice versa. A central communication hub for all LPs does not yet exist.

Wholesaling to other producers is great brand marketing. Your cannabis will be distributed far and wide and your product will speak for you in repeat orders. As a producer, you also have the discretion of offering your clients direct-to-market prices, able to charge $2 to $6 per gram. You may keep your small and growing clientele happy as a short-term gain. If you decide to sell your cannabis wholesale in the future, your direct-to-market prices may need to be re-strategized, which could cause some of your clients to leave in desperation or, worse, anger. Having a long-term plan in mind will avoid harsh changes in marketing and pricing.

A model similar to a business improvement association is useful. Cannabis Growers of Canada is, according to its site (cannagrowers.ca), "an association of cannabis businesses in Canada that are dedicated to building a free and fair craft cannabis economy." The Canadian Association of Medical Cannabis Dispensaries (camcd.ca) is another example.

The ACMPR continues to be a work in progress as it is not perfectly square with the Canadian Charter. As a result, small changes will happen over time. As a burgeoning or successful LP you should consider contributing to various legal challenges or political opportunities that could bring about substantial positive change.

A reputation for high-quality service, products, or strains is the best advertising. It will set you apart from your competitors as well as from Big Cannabis. You do not need to be the producer of high-quality cannabis to be known as the go-to person for reliable sources or services. If you think of the number and variety of microbrewed beers and the hundreds of related services, you will understand the vastness of these uncharted opportunities.

Your marketing materials cannot make any medical or health claims. There are limited traditional advertising opportunities under the *Cannabis Act* but similar to alcohol and tobacco, knowledge of the legislation and creativity is key.

The saying "know thyself" is true in that you should develop a small number of high-quality products, get really good at those and know them well, before tackling larger challenges or numerous products.

Expect to spend 15 to 33 percent of your budget on marketing. Proper brand marketing is critical. Reputation and brand is everything in the cannabis industry.

1. Name and Logo

In the beginning, as you plan your business, pick a company name and logo. Make sure you are insanely proud of both. This pride should carry over into your day-to-day work and it is then reflected in the quality of the cannabis, service, or product you deliver. Having a great brand, a great team, and a great work environment is a rare thing and requires almost daily attention on the part of the team leader.

Make sure your name is original because if someone else is using the same one (or one too similar to it), you may not be able to obtain all of the trademarks you will need as a legal business entity.

Consult a specialist to create and execute a marketing strategy and business plan. Good websites for obtaining your basic graphic art needs are 99designs.ca or fiverr.com. There are marketing agencies that specialize in brand identity; they may charge $5,000 to $50,000 depending on your scope and needs.

A brand identity can be sent over in a custom multipage file that displays your corporate colors, fonts, layouts, and images. There is also a technical graphic design breakdown of your logo. You should be able to hand this document to a competent designer who will know how to adapt your brand identity elements into any new marketing or design project. Consistent use of your corporate identity elements should be a cornerstone of your marketing.

2. Social Networking

Social networking opportunities to promote your brand are endless and have no ceiling in costs. Know your customers, how they like to communicate, and what makes them happy, and cater to that. Build a marketing strategy around these variables.

Your website must be easy to navigate, join, and place an order, if you're able to sell online. Allowing your customers to provide direct feedback to you can provide you with invaluable information.

The online basic necessities include a well-designed website, merchant account, Facebook, and Twitter. Consult with a social networking expert, or recent university student, to explain its long-term value and how to maximize these opportunities.

Many social media platforms forbid the marketing of narcotics, which includes cannabis. This applies worldwide including states that have legalized cannabis. Your account can be frozen or deleted if you break end-user agreements. The appeals processes or departments on these platforms are often poorly staffed and tedious and rarely result in a positive outcome.

The easiest way to understand the use of social media and your specific project is to see what other people have done. If you want to invest your time and money into extractions or specialty chocolates, for example, there are hundreds of brands in Canada and the US using accounts on Facebook, Instagram, Twitter, and Snapchat. Hashtags are critical to proper use of social media as it will more effectively transmit your brand and allow you to be found. Look for accounts that have 25,000 subscribers or more and copy what they do. There are also websites and apps that will help you find the most popular hashtags.

Some of the more popular hashtags in 2017 were #highsociety #iwillmarrymary #ostf #710 #420 #cannabis #highlife #kush.

Emojis and giphys are also good tools, especially when marketing to the 18 to 25 demographic. YouTube has endless videos on the use of both of them.

Social media maintenance is a bit of specialty and a bit of lifestyle in that it requires regular daily maintenance, analysis of types and volumes of responses, and an awareness of trends and efficiencies within each platform. Different demographics appeal to different platforms. The easiest way to find out what platforms your customers are using is to communicate directly with each client, ideally in person, or new clients as they sign up.

Despite the benefits of social media, face-to-face communication still has the highest possible bandwidth with the best possibilities to build long-term relationships. Telephone calls are a distant second.

The goal of any business social media account, in my opinion, is to grow it. In retail, you might decide you want to obtain 10,000 subscribers. You will need to employ several strategies to attain this goal, which requires some research (YouTube) and networking. Once you have reached your goal, you may decide to reassess your marketing and focus to mature your account to 25,000 subscribers.

3. Search Engines

Search Engine Optimization (SEO) is critical to your website being found on most search engines. It is also a specialty within the world of web marketing, in that the rules of how SEO works most efficiently change a little bit every few months, while substantial changes come every couple of years. These substantial changes may require small or large changes or occasionally an overhaul of your SEO strategies. Is the copy on your website descriptive enough? Do enough high-ranking websites link to yours? There are so many variables that can affect where your site shows up in the listings.

In the search engine world, you can also pay for placement through Google AdWords or other search engines, which will allow you to bid a maximum amount per clickthrough. Essentially you can pay to have people come to your site through your ads. This requires much maintenance as well, to ensure you're not going over budget, that you're getting clickthroughs, and that enough of them are converting into sales to make your return on investment profitable.

Another form of advertising which is more passive monetizes your web hits: third party advertising banners on your site. A banner ad placed on your website, for example, would pay you based on the number of advertising impressions. This advertising block is paid in cost per thousand (CPM).

It is important to note that search engines such as Google may still consider cannabis illegal, and you may violate the end-user agreement even if you are not promoting a cannabis product directly.

4. Blogging

Much like travel bloggers have successfully converted their hobby into revenue, cannabis blogging could be as attractive. Your only goal is to grow your viewership to 25,000 subscribers or more. You can focus on the aspects of the cannabis industry that inspire and interest you. I picked 25,000 because it is a number that approaches the ability for an individual to sustain themselves financially, if executed correctly and wisely. Depending on level of community engagement and virality it could be substantially less than 25,000. Your content will not survive if you are constantly selling something — whereas constantly promoting your web store and sharing links is acceptable and commonly done.

Here are some of the topics I have seen bloggers cover: What products are LPs selling, current events in news, legislation or by-laws, financial analysis and trading of cannabis stocks, photography, comedy, dispensaries, local politics, music, yoga, cannabis gardens, celebrities, regional cannabis events, and extracts, just to name a few.

The sky really is the limit; follow your passions and interests and share it with the world. Yes, you can have more than one facet to your social media content. Your only requirements are that your content is relevant, interesting, and fresh. In the end, as long as it's speaking to your customers, the people spending money at your business, it's doing its job.

I have seen some bloggers who are "personalities," so if you, or someone you know, is the life of the party or has a certain charisma, and is committed to producing regular content, consider whether this person would be able to —

- create at least three original pieces of content each week,

- produce 15 to 40 minutes of audio content once per week, and/or

- produce two to ten minutes of video content once every week.

Spend some time each week engaging with similar bloggers via their social media channels. They should have a larger subscription base than you to help you grow yours, if possible. Copying what they do will teach you different strategies that will carry you to 25,000 subscribers and beyond.

5. Web Conversions

Whether you are marketing from social media or from a website, you must calculate your conversion rate, or the amount of sales you are getting directly through those online channels. This will give you valuable information about whether what you are doing is working.

If your website matures to 25,000 visits in a month (or 25,000 subscribers), and you have sold 300 orders, then your conversion rate is 1.2 percent. You can further calculate your average sale per order. You should be on the constant lookout for what can you do to improve your conversion rate and average sale amount.

You should also consider how many people are researching your company online but then showing up in person to purchase and comparing online sales versus sales that occur fully in-store. This will give you a better idea of how well your website and web marketing is working.

6. Advertising

There are limits on advertising in the cannabis industry in Canada. Cannabis is still considered a narcotic. The Canadian Narcotics Control Regulations states: "advertisement means any representation by any means whatever for the purpose of promoting directly or indirectly the sale or disposal of a narcotic."

As things become legal in more jurisdictions, it is likely that you will still not be allowed to have big posters advertising cannabis that children can see. As with cigarettes in Canada, I doubt you'll be allowed to do traditional types of advertising.

In the US, all advertising of narcotics including cannabis and cannabis products is illegal under federal law, although certain states will allow some forms of advertising. For example, in Washington, there are billboards on the side of the I-5 advertising cannabis shops in the area. As with everything to do with the cannabis business at this time, be sure to check the laws in your area before investing in advertisements.

As with all marketing, think about how best to identify and target your audience with any advertising you plan to do.

As mentioned in Chapter 8, if you are running a retail location, you might consider creating a concise handbill explaining the rules to tourists in your area. See Sample 1 for a flyer I imagine one might use once cannabis is legal in Canada.

7. Packaging

Legalization, no matter where you are, means that there are likely going to be minimum standards on packaging for wholesale and retail.

All medical cannabis should be retailed with a label that clearly states what is inside the container. In Canada, medical cannabis can only be mailed and the cannabis itself must be in a childproof container. Expect each state and province to have different standards about how things must be labeled so again, this is another place you must do your research depending on where you plan to do business.

Storing cannabis in nitrogen filled or vacuum packaging will extend the shelf life of cannabis, as could refrigeration. As mentioned previously, some LED lights inside the boxes when shipping plants can help avoid the flowering process from beginning before they are ready.

Of course, you should also consider the attractiveness of packaging, as from a marketing standpoint, your packaging represents your product and your business. Talk to graphic designers, decide how your business logo can go on your packaging and how to best accomplish all the legal requirements while still packaging products in a way that pleases the eye.

Welcome to Canada, where cannabis is legal!

Dos and Don'ts while consuming cannabis in Canada:

- Do consume small amounts of cannabis at a time.

- Do not buy cannabis from people you don't know well. Avoid street dealers.

- Do not possess more than 30g of cannabis or 7.5g of concentrates at any one time.

- Do not consume edibles alone, especially for first timers. Do follow dosing information for edibles.

- If you consume too much cannabis, ask for a "come-down" product, available at some hemp stores, cannabis retailers, and online.

- Do not consume cannabis near childrens' parks, schools, etc.

- Do not mix cannabis and alcohol.

- Do not drive if you are impaired with cannabis.

- Do not resell your cannabis.

- Do not leave Canada with cannabis in your possession.

Note: Sample 1 is something you might use when cannabis is legal.

21
Special Events, Trade Shows, and Conferences

Now that cannabis is about to be legal in Canada and other countries, you can market your brand at special events, or even create your own special event that celebrates cannabis and cannabis culture. This is an opportunity to make your brand shine by showing how you stand out and what is special about your organization.

You can be a vendor, promoter, sponsor, or attendee of these events to promote your brand. Examples of special events are outdoor music festivals, rib events, chili cook-offs, cancer fundraisers, AIDS-related fundraisers, MS events, food markets, trade shows, and garden shows.

It is not clear how events will work under Canada's *Cannabis Act*, with cannabis being considered something to be controlled in the same kind of way alcohol is only served to adults in a beer garden.

Trade shows related to personal health are target-rich environments for potential medical cannabis users. They provide information sharing and networking opportunities with other healthcare workers and organizations. If you are reading this book, then you must also understand the value of educating the public and other medical professionals on the benefits of using therapeutic cannabis and cannabinoids. Growing the industry is the responsibility of all active parties.

Creating strategic relationships with other LPs will be critical to your success by shoring up your weaknesses and boosting your strengths. Figuring out how you can help other LPs, and how other LPs can help you will be a large part of finding your team's circle of influence — and your place in the cannabis industry.

Cannabis conferences come in different types: business based (business to customer or business to business) and academic based. They are sometimes combined, but the festive waft of cannabis seems to create an environment that is counterproductive to any short-term academic and corporate goals of the conference.

Trade show events are fairly festive and are great venues for meeting industry players both big and small. Some events have several hundred vendors providing almost everything imaginable related to cannabis, and sometimes not so related. You should attend at least one of these events every other year to study how other organizations are effectively branding and marketing, stay plugged into current events, maintain good domestic and foreign relations, and see what is not yet available in your home country.

The highest quality is not always with the biggest brand. Buying and selling in wholesale quantities are easily arranged at these events with the right licensing. Once you go to a few of these events you will understand their full value and where your brand could or would belong. The following are some events to consider attending:

- Spannabis takes place every February in Barcelona: spannabis.com

- *High Times* magazine puts on the Cannabis Cup every November (on American Thanksgiving weekend) in Los Angeles, San Francisco, and Colorado: cannabiscup.com

- Seattle Hempfest has the largest outdoor cannabis event: hempfest.org

- Toronto has an annual two-day Global Marijuana March (GMM) in early May. About 40,000 people attend each day: globalmarijuanamarch.com. There are more than 200 cities participating in the GMM first started by Dana Beal in NYC. GMMs take place on the first or second weekend of every May. See cannabis.shoutwiki.com/wiki/Global_Marijuana_ March for participating cities.

- *Denver Post* listed no fewer than 13 separate events for 420 in the year 2017. This is proof that cannabis and cannabis events are big business.

Academic conferences tend be less festive than trade shows and focus more on the medical studies and presentations. Attending academic conferences is ideal for developing IP and the continuing education of any doctors, pharmacists, or nurse-practitioners you have on staff. Most professionals' colleges require 20 to 75 hours per year of continuing education credits. These conferences usually satisfy some of those credit requirements. You are likely to see at least one representative from every major pharmaceutical corporation there. The International Association for Cannabinoids as Medicine is a good place to start. There are several similar international research organizations as well:

- British Pharmacological Society's European Workshop on Cannabinoid Research: www.bps.ac.uk/news-events/future-scientific-meetings/past-meetings/8th-european-workshop-on-cannabinoid-research#

- The Canadian Consortium for the Investigation of Cannabinoids: www.ccic.net

- CannMed (American): www.cannmedevents.com

- International Conference on Medical Cannabis and Cannabinoids: medical-cannabis-conference.com

- International Cannabinoid Research Society: icrs.co

Every month, there is at least one conference in the world regarding medical cannabis.

Annual trade shows in Amsterdam, Barcelona, Colorado, Washington, and California will be enormously useful for collecting sales and marketing information from all over the world. These shows are especially useful for small- to mid-sized medical companies with strong IP strategies.

You can also create a type of farmers' market for handmade cannabis and hemp crafts. Revenues come from door fees and vendors tables fees primarily. This is a great way to meet and network with other craft or cottage industry producers. Depending on the laws, markets can sell whole cannabis and extracts, while others may sell non-psychoactive products only.

22
Networking and
Neighborhood Marketing

Staying in regular communication with others in the industry, whether through associations and/or your own networking, will be critical to staying on top of new developments and strategies. Learning how other businesses deal with different situations will help you to avoid making costly mistakes. Forming and maintaining high-quality relationships with small and large businesses and entrepreneurs is key to any long-term success.

Cannabis Canada (cann-can.ca) is an association for Licensed Producers in Canada; should you become an LP in Canada, I suggest you join to stay on top of industry trends and to network. Also see the download kit included with this book for links to other associations and groups.

It needs to be said that when you're opening a business that deals in cannabis, there may be some people who don't agree with what you're doing. Most of the time this won't be your problem, but sometimes, maybe it's a next-door neighbor in your shopping plaza who really dislikes your business. It doesn't hurt to introduce yourself around any neighborhood before you open up shop so the neighbors know you're not to be feared and your business is legal and legit. A little kindness and relationship building can go a long way.

If you are complying with all laws and regulations, there isn't much damage that can result from any complaint.

23
Your Team (HR) and Your Security (Cyber and Physical)

1. Your Team (HR)

Depending on your long-term goals, your team should include some or all of these business skills or specialties as part of the LP business:

- Executive direction

- Administration and communications

- Security

- Compliance and quality assurance

- Analysis

- Finance

- Import/export

- Legal

- Sales

- Marketing

- IT and web

- Bookkeeping and/or accounting

Ideally, team members will have skills in more than one area; overlap will help you fill holes with a leaner team. Be wary of spreading your resources too thin which can be tempting for the chronic multitasker. Identifying specific roles your team lacks will help you determine what roles will need to be outsourced; this is important in planning your operational budget.

If you have an ambitious plan, you should consider a management team, consisting of experienced Chief Executive Officer, Chief Financial Officer, Chief Operations Officer, etc. Consider all of this when you draft a business plan (see Chapter 24).

If you will be taking on the initial hirings (and maybe even firings) yourself, be sure to look up labor laws in your area. Know what you're legally allowed to ask an interviewee, and what you are allowed to expect of an employee.

Research where to post job openings; ideally in places people experienced in the cannabis industry will find them.

Health Canada or state laws may dictate that employees in the cannabis industry must have clean criminal records (or some other stipulation) so be sure to learn what you legally need to look for or avoid. If you've never interviewed, hired, or managed people before, now is a good time to read some books on the subject.

2. Your Security (Cyber and Physical)

Security is an important part of the cannabis business. As far as trade secrets, personal and business information go, make sure you use different passwords on different sites; enable a firewall and antivirus software; and generally be sure to protect what you've got.

After all, this is your business, and potentially, the private, medical information of your clients.

In some areas, there may even be laws around how you protect this information and secure your product, so research this as well.

As far as physical security, given that cannabis used to be a cash-only business, and banks and credit card companies didn't want to touch us, a lot of us will be used to dealing in cash, hiring security guards, and having an alarm service and a cash safe. Until money from cannabis businesses is accepted at all banks and legal everywhere, these things will still come into play in some way, and even when it's all legal, security guards and alarms may be necessary as cannabis will still be desired, cost money, and potentially that will mean someone will want to steal it or any cash you have.

Think about this, and also about basic safety issues, such as whether to use deadbolt locks on the doors, bars on windows, and motion-sensor lights and cameras in parking and entry areas to keep staff, customers, and product safe.

24.
Writing a Business Plan

Writing a business plan serves several critical functions. It clearly explains your vision and business model and shows that your plan is supported by financial projections.

It explains who and what you have, what you will need and why, and what you are offering in exchange for investments or loans.

There are thousands of websites, videos, and apps to assist you in writing your business plan. Some people specialize in writing business plans, such as these variations:

- **Detailed business plan:** Your detailed business plan should be many pages long and it is very private because it should contain personal contact information, banking details, and intimate explanation of your business model and financials.

- **Public business plan:** This is a condensed version of the detailed business plan containing information you want to give to investors. You will probably customize your documents for specific investors by expanding or taking away content relevant to your meetings.

- **Investment deck:** Investment decks are a brief explanation of what your project is about; generally, an 8- to 25-page PowerPoint presentation that encapsulates the who, what, when, where, and why of your investment plan. It should include additional pages that show adequate financial projections to support your vision and business models.

Some people write the investment deck first which helps to flush out the broad strokes of your vision. There are different ways of approaching a business plan. Find the way that works best for you and your team and use it regularly as it is an invaluable tool to have.

Writing a SWOT analysis as part of your detailed plan is also useful as it is a concise document that details your Strengths, Weaknesses, Opportunities, and Threats, usually in point form:

- **Strengths:** What are your brand's strengths?

- **Weaknesses:** What are your brand's weaknesses?

- **Opportunities:** What short- and long-term opportunities is your brand pursuing?

- **Threats:** What are the hazards and pitfalls in your pursuit of success?

SWOT analysis should not be part of every investment deck but certainly part of the business plan.

Success is your goal but thinking about your eventual exit strategy will change the nature of how you approach your business. As an entrepreneur, your goal is to grow your business to be the biggest fish possible. The pond will be very busy with other fish of different sizes in a few years so getting in early is key to growing successfully. As you go forward, you will need to acquire assets in order to scale your successful business to new levels. This is accomplished in several ways depending on your needs and goals:

- Your organization partners with another organization of a similar size.

- Your organization absorbs a smaller organization.

- Your organization gets absorbed by a larger organization.

Given that Shoppers Drug Mart (a national pharmacy brand) in Canada will be a major distributor of medical cannabis, it is conceivable that in the future mega corporations such as Monsanto, Marlborough, LVMH, will jump in the game. As time goes on, it will likely become more difficult for medical boutique operations to compete against established brands. Always be on the lookout for good dance partners in business so that you can find a niche or keep your competitive edge.

See Sample 2 for a business plan template. It is also included on the download kit that came with this book for you to start planning your venture.

Sample 2
Business Plan

This template is a starting point for you to create your business plan. It is important you begin this process well before launching your business. Write your mission statement last, as it needs to encompass the whole idea for your business and will be easier to write when you have thought through the rest.

Think through and fill in each section for your business.

OWNERS

Your Name: _____

Address 1: _____

Address 2: _____

City, State/Province, Zip Code/Postal Code: _____

Phone Number: _____

Email: _____

Name of Company: _____

Projected Start Date: _____

Business Number or Employer Identification Number (if available): _____

Mission Statement

Write this section last. Make it a short and sweet snapshot of the business explaining who you will sell to, your role, where you will sell services, what will spell success to you, why people should hire you, and how you will sell yourself to clients.

Vision Statement and Company Description:

This is a broad and inspirational statement that discusses size, structure, and influence of your business in the future: Your vision for the company. Think about:

Who is involved and what experience do they bring to this venture?

What market will you serve in the industry?

What changes do you foresee for your industry in the long and short term?

Where do you see your business in five years? Ten?

When do you plan on expanding?

Why does your industry need another business?

How do you measure success in your business?

How will your business deal with growth and change?

Sample 2 - continued

Structure and Management:

Think about whether your company is to be a sole proprietorship/partnership/ corporation providing services to local and regional individuals, and businesses.

> *Who will be your accountant, board members, banker, insurance agent, mentors?*
>
> *Who will be employed by the company?*
>
> *What management style will you practice?*
>
> *Where will you find the right employees?*
>
> *When will employees get paid?*
>
> *Why you will have employees instead of contracted individuals, or vice versa?*
>
> *How will schedules and procedures be prepared and shared?*

Elevator Speech:

Make this no longer than 60 seconds, mention your business name several times throughout the speech, use visual and descriptive words, end with a tag line of five to ten words maximum.

Think:

> *Who are your target markets?*
>
> *What exactly do you do?*
>
> *When did you enter the industry?*
>
> *Why are you superior to your competition?*
>
> *How do your services make the client's life easier?*

Products and Services:

What services will you provide in the next 12 months, how long do you estimate it will take to execute for each element you will offer of your business?

Think about:

> *Who is your target market?*
>
> *What is your estimated life cycle of products provided?*
>
> *Where will your services be marketed (have photos, brochures, advertisements and other in appendix)?*
>
> *How will your product have a competitive advantage or disadvantage in industry?*

Industry Overview:

> *Who is currently your industry leader and biggest competition, locally and globally?*
>
> *What are average pricing structures like in your market?*
>
> *When is your product highly in demand?*
>
> *Where is your niche, or unique share in the market?*
>
> *How will you overcome barriers to entry?*

Sample 2 - continued

Marketing Plan:

Who is your target market?

What is your sales and promotion strategy?

Where will you brand your company and where will you take it logistically?

When do you plan to implement these plans?

Why are your methods of marketing going to be successful?

How will you brand the company to be recognizable to clients?

Regulatory Issues:

Who may you need to have nondisclosure agreements with?

What requirements does your business structure entail?

What are the zoning or building requirements?

When are applications and deadlines for regulatory forms?

How many permits and licenses are required for your business to start up?

Risk Plan:

What are potential services or products you can't provide?

Where will you document failures and your follow-up to these?

When will you determine your business is at risk?

Why do you think your business will ever be at risk?

How will you measure what risks your business is currently facing?

Operational Plan:

Describe your location, equipment, people, processes, and surroundings.

Where will you have your business?

Who will need access to your location?

What will be your structure to monitor quality control?

When will your business be open?

Why did you choose certain equipment and processes?

How will your products be provided to the client?

Financial Plan:

Who is liable for business finances?

What are the personal financial statements of the owners?

Where do you project your business profit projection to be in 12 months? Two years?

What are your assumptions about projected cash flow?

How will your payment plan affect your cash flow and inventory?

Start-up Expenses and Plan:

How much do you need for start-up and when does start-up begin and end?

Who will front the start-up costs and what percentage ownership will he or she hold?

What will expenses be?

What is your contingency plan?

Investment Plan:

Do you have the money or do you need additional financing or loans? Where will you seek the money?

What are your projected sales and expenses?

How much profit do you expect?

Where will you open your business bank account?

When will you break even?

Pricing and Payment:

Will you be taking cash, credit, check, PayPal?

Will you be invoicing clients and what will your terms be?

Appendices:

Include as much of the following as you can to back up what you said throughout the business plan:

- Brochures and marketing materials including logo
- Personal financial statements
- Start-up cost details
- SWOT analysis
- Photos and maps of office location
- Detailed list of office equipment needed
- Copies of business documents, leases, and contracts
- Industry-related articles that support what you want to do
- Book references to research
- Detailed market research
- Letters of support from past or future potential customers
- Letters of referral from colleagues
- Your biography and experience (a résumé)

Part 3
Canada-Specific Cannabis Business

The following chapters will delve into cannabis issues that are Canada-specific. If you are looking for US-only information please see Part 4.

25
Canada-Specific Cannabis

In 2000, Canadian Federal Health Minister Alan Rock announced that Prairie Plant Systems (PPS) had been awarded the only federal contract to produce dried cannabis. When Anne McClellan became Minister of Health in 2002, she stated that the cannabis grown by Prairie Plant Systems was research grade and not fit for public consumption. Several licensed users launched a lawsuit against the Government of Canada to access this cannabis and they won. There were fewer than 100 Authorizations to Possess (ATPs), in Canada at this time.

Medical users were said to find the quality substandard, containing bits of stem and leaf; low potency; exposed to radiation and generally unacceptable in taste, aroma, and effect. A small number of lawsuits and criminal cases against the Government of Canada resulted in the Medical Marihuana Access Regulations (MMAR).

The MMAR was designed to meet the immediate needs of ATPs by allowing them to grow for themselves or have one person grow for them. That grower could grow for one ATP only. This is referred to as the one-to-one rule — 1:1 — and it effectively bottlenecked the industry. Thousands of Canadians wanted to legitimately, and sometimes illegitimately, produce medical cannabis in a legal environment.

In 2002, a case called *Sfetkopoulos v. Canada* challenged, among other things, the 1:1 rule calling it unconstitutional for some of the following reasons:

- Litigants argued for cost of production; it is cheaper and easier to grow a 1,000 plants in one location rather than 10 plants in 100 locations.

- There is no rationale behind the 1:1 rule because there is no constitutional reason for it and it doesn't address knowledge, materials, plants, and testing.

- The regulations were written as if everyone has an uncle that knows how to grow it.

The judge and appellate courts agreed that there was no constitutional reason to limit growers to one patient.

In response to several court decisions, Health Canada increased the rule to 2:1 — just barely enough to make business viable, but not enough to create a self-sustaining industry. Police forces and municipalities across Canada were dismayed to find legal grow-ops of 20 to 500 plants in their jurisdictions. They were also powerless to stop them as they were operating in accordance with Health Canada's MMAR regulations.

In April 2013, the new Marihuana for Medical Purposes Regulations (MMPR) took effect and were in full force by April 2014. The MMPR is a surprisingly positive step forward as it removes the regulatory bottleneck imposed by the 2:1 rule. While there are substantial issues that remain unresolved, the regulations break new ground in that they cover every aspect of the plant from seed to harvest to analysis to distribution; each aspect and transaction requires proper documentation in an audit-ready framework. Licensed production is now a serious administrative effort. This means you can expect staff to spend at least 10 percent of their time on documentation alone.

Canada could become a world leader in this highly promising industry. The regulations are a good start, but the majority of the effort will have to come from within the industry and not from the government.

Canada also has a distinct advantage over individual American states that have legalized or medicalized their cannabis industry, such as Colorado, Washington, California; cross-state issues aside, the US federal government is at strong political odds with these state initiatives. Although state rights versus federal rights will be argued in the court systems, federal agencies such as the DEA, IRS, FPO, ATF, DHS, and FBI remain powerful and entitled federal tools. These agencies can and do work together to bear down on well-meaning entrepreneurs, and do so with extreme prejudice.

Canada's ACMPR and the *Cannabis Act* are strikingly different. It is national legislation affecting federal, provincial, and municipal governments, agencies, and policies which must now adapt to comply with federal regulations. To do otherwise, or resist federal policies, could violate the Charter of Rights. This decision puts Canada at the world forefront for progressive drug policy and many countries are looking at Canada's execution of policy and its results.

Canada has a comparative can-do full-commerce approach to cannabis versus the American state-by-state approach, with its inherent limitations on banking, taxation, and inter-state commerce. These US limitations are also a substantial risk as they could fall under the jurisdiction of national drug enforcement agencies. The Canadian approach is not without criticism but it is certainly a step in the right direction.

The ACMPR allows for corporations to be licensed. The commercial production license granted to a corporation would extend to its staff provided they are supervised properly as specified under the ACMPR. This creates the possibility for dozens or hundreds of working staff under a single production license.

The ACMPR does prohibit commercial growing in dwellings for personal production, and designated production. The current Authorization To Possess (ATP) process will be replaced with a prescription-type process. This is a substantial change for those ATPs growing their own cannabis under the MMAR. Licensed production can no longer be an enterprise two or three industrious university students can pull off easily in their basements. There are many challenging facets to the regulations. Understanding and mastering these challenges will guide you to further opportunities domestically and abroad.

1. The Emerging Industry in Canada

Big Cannabis has come. The race is on. The market has, in a few short years, been dominated by a handful of brands and they will occupy the large advertising spaces and employ glossy spokespeople — they will be hard to ignore, like, say, Labatt and Molson in the beer industry.

So where does the ambitious enthusiast belong in this industry that will soon be filled with big companies?

The cannabis industry is not exactly new. It borrows a little from the alcohol, tobacco, candy/soda, advertising, dot-com, pharmaceutical, and food industries. As new opportunities come up, new business models emerge that relate to one or more of these existing industries. There is rarely the need to recreate the wheel. There are important lessons to be learned from each of these parallel industries. With many players already in the field, do not be intimidated — you can succeed with enough innovation and resourcefulness.

Let's continue to use the beer industry as a model. While Labatt and Molson dominate the Canadian beer industry, there is nonetheless a thriving and lucrative micro- and craft-brewing industry; the reason for this simple, people have always, and will always want more options, specialties, more flavors — bespoke experiences. The Canadian brewing behemoths do not waste resources trying to compete with every craft brewer — they understand that it just cannot be done. The beer market is big enough for both subindustries to coexist. Each subindustry is worth billions of dollars each year.

Here is a list of some of the jobs in the beer industry. You will see that there should be — or are — equivalent jobs in the cannabis industry, but the legal cannabis industry itself is too new to contain all of the possible jobs the beer industry has, at least right now.

• Master brewer

- Brew master
- Brew technician
- Quality assurance
- Compliance
- Safety officer (WHIMS)
- Bottling, packaging, and labeling
- Marketing, promotions, online presence, merchandising
- Events and events management
- Equipment maintenance
- Security
- Security equipment setup and maintenance
- Human resources
- Supply management
- Distributors
- Information technology
- Transport
- Retail
- Dial-a-bottle or home-delivery service
- Bartender
- Bar manager
- School (teachers) to certify bartenders
- Bookkeeping and payroll
- Accounting
- Unions and union representatives
- Insurance provider
- Legal: trademark and copyright

- Industry financing

- Lobbyists

If you have enough resourcefulness to market your craft products, you can successfully tap into a multibillion-dollar industry, but not easily. A well-organized, moderately-funded husband-wife, or two- or three-person team should be able to start something small that can grow into something big, just like your favorite plant!

For any level of government to exclude the craft industry would not only be a failure of true legalization, but also a disservice to the many individuals who fought in the court system to create a societal environment that is finally open to the idea that cannabis use is a normal adult behavior and should be legalized on that basis.

To put things in perspective, it is legal as of this writing for anyone in Canada to grow 15 kg of tobacco per year per household (laws-lois.justice.gc.ca/eng/acts/E-14.1/page-4.html#docCont).

Health Canada initially estimated licensing around 200 producers in the first two years of the program. After four years there are fewer than 100. Health Canada also initially estimated there would be 50,000 medical cannabis users, nationwide, in that same time period. If 50,000 licensed medical users use an average of 5 grams per day this means that the national supply will be 250 kg per day or more than 91,000 kg per year. Those 50,000 medical users represent less than 4 percent of Canadians who use medical cannabis. There are currently about 275,000 medical cannabis users.

Health Canada also estimates that by 2024 there will be 430,000 licensed medical users. Using the same 5 grams per day average, it is the equivalent to 2,150 kg per day or 785,000 kg per year for medical use only. The market is currently undersaturated and nowhere near critical mass.

2. How to Approach Health Canada Regulations

Reading hundreds of pages of policy and regulations is daunting work, more so for the uninitiated. Having a lawyer on your team would be very helpful, although costly. Gather a list of questions while reading the ACMPR, the *Cannabis Act,* and this book, so when the executive meetings happen, everyone's time is maximized. Here are a few topics to cover in those meetings:

- Pre-licensing issues
- Real estate/location
- Applying for a license
- Risks
- Costs
- Financing
- Procedures
- Business structure
- Share allotment
- Accounting
- Security
- Compliance
- Analysis
- Insurance

It is unlikely that your team will have all of the skills required to make an application. You will likely need the help of one or more consultants to guide you through various stages of approval.

In the preamble before the proposed MMPR (which preceded the ACMPR) regulations (*Canada Gazette* December 15, 2012), the sections labeled "Objectives" and "Background" are the short version of the MMPR. These four pages cover the entire scope of the program. Writing these details as policy was no easy task, which explains why the MMPR and ACMPR are sizeable documents. See the download kit for links to applicable laws.

If you have trouble understanding the regulations at first, do not worry. Try to skim through it a few times especially if this is your first time reading legislation and policies. Try to discuss the ACMPR and *Cannabis Act* with other people on your team, people you know who want to be in the cannabis industry, or online.

When reading regulations, I have found it beneficial to be online and have multiple windows and tabs open so that I can cross reference information. If you find yourself doing this, it is a good sign that you are learning the skill of reading legislation and policy. See Figure 1.

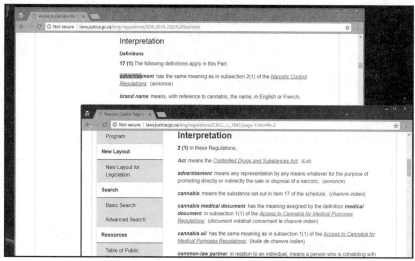

Figure 1: Screenshot of More Than One Tab Open

The writers at Health Canada have made efforts to write the regulations in plain, easy-to-read English and French. Reading it from start to finish may be hard to digest and the document is daunting; however, good familiarity and thorough understanding of the ACMPR and the *Cannabis Act* is critical to unlocking any opportunities, as well as the subsequent plan of execution.

3. Health Canada-Related Documents

As a potential canna-business person, or Licensed Producer (LP), you must be very familiar, not only with the ACMPR and the *Cannabis Act*, but also with these other Health Canada-related documents:

- Directive on Physical Security Requirements for Controlled Substances

- Building and Production Security Requirements for Marihuana for Medical Purposes

- Technical Specifications for Dried Marihuana for Medical Purposes

Government of Canada acts or regulations that you will need to reference:

- *Food and Drug Act* (FDA)

- *Narcotics Control Regulations* (NCR)

- *Controlled Drugs and Substances Act* (CDSA)

Each of these documents is enormous but you will only need to read and absorb specific sections within them.

Most of these documents can be found through healthcanada. gc.ca/mma or by searching the documents' names in a search engine. All Government of Canada websites end in ".gc.ca."

26
Medical Cannabis in Canada

According to the Access to Cannabis for Medical Purposes Regulations (ACMPR), getting access to cannabis is relatively easy, provided the patient qualifies and the applicant's physician will sign a one-page form. Finding a Healthcare Practitioner (HCP) is getting easier with the many clinics offering medical cannabis services. However, it is less easy for the HCPs if the applicants are not their regular patients.

When providing a diagnosis, the physician may need to be a related specialist or the applicant must have already seen a related specialist. A family practitioner, also known as general practitioner (GP) can sign the necessary form if the patient has already been seen by a related specialist. Physicians, like most professionals, tend to be more risk-averse than nonprofessionals. Addressing risks or other profession issues to each HCP's satisfaction will not be easy; however, it is required if you wish to do business with a physician directly.

Qualifying as a medical user means being diagnosed with criteria listed in one or both of the Diagnostic and Statistical Manual (DSM) or the International Classification of Diseases (ICD-10). It does cover mainstream illnesses such as cancer, HIV, arthritis, epilepsy, etc. It also covers lesser known conditions such as migraines, sleep disorders, PMS, depression, and much more. A quick online review of the DSM and ICD-10 will help you gain greater clarity on this business facet.

The physician's due diligence and ability to qualify an applicant is governed by his or her provincial medical college — not by Health Canada and not by the ACMPR. See the download kit for a sample List of Possible Diagnoses.

The ACMPR stipulates that the following information must be included in a medical document signed and dated by the health-care practitioner:

- Patient's full name, patient's date of birth, gender

- Address where the patient consulted with the practitioner

- Daily grams of dried marihuana per day to be used by the patient

- Health-care practitioner's name and his or her administrative information

- An attestation by the health-care practitioner that the information contained in the document is correct and complete

- Location for the assessment if it was not performed at the physician's office

When medical users obtain the forms from the signing physicians, they must then register with the LP of their choice if they choose not to grow for themselves. You can pick more than one LP; however, the daily amount must be divided by the number of LPs selected. The physician must send a signed medical document to notify the appropriate LP(s) to commence distribution. The signing HCP may have a business relationship with specific LPs or more likely to the clinic. There should be no hiding this fact on the part of the physician or the clinic, especially if asked directly.

Once a person has received a first order from an LP, he or she will be considered a 100 percent legal medical cannabis user. The container the cannabis is shipped in is essentially a prescription bottle and it acts as proof of medical status. This will come in handy if there are any law enforcement issues or when consuming medical cannabis in public.

If you are fortunate enough to grow your retail client base to a few hundred clients, you will be within reach of doing a full but small study. Studies can be a corporate opportunity (revenue stream), which could lead to larger studies, as well as developing IP, and DIN-approved products or medical devices. It is also a good use of resources. Studies have hundreds of variables and goals. A physician or medical researcher can assist you in developing a road map. You will need to consult with an IP lawyer at an early phase of development.

The ability to create and execute studies (consulting) for other LPs could prove to be a valuable skill (revenue stream).

1. Becoming a Medical Cannabis User in Canada

If someone is more than a casual consumer of cannabis, I would strongly recommend obtaining a Health Canada medical license to possess and/or cultivate, especially if you are diagnosed with a chronic or terminal condition. Here is why. With a license:

- You have a right to consume your medical cannabis anywhere you can consume tobacco. As a recreational user you may be banned from consuming cannabis in public spaces. This will vary from province to province and not all the rules have been set yet.

- Your work space is supposed to designate a space for you to consume your medicine (see *Canadians with Disabilities Act*).

- You can grow more than four plants at one time in a single residence

- You can possess more than the recreational limit of 30 g of cannabis (depends on physician prescription).

- You can possess more than the recreational limit of 7.5 g of concentrates (depends on physician prescription).

- You can possess all forms of cannabis. The *Cannabis Act* does not allow for extracts and edibles yet. Each province will decide when they will be made available to the public.

- It is not clear if consuming medical cannabis and driving is a convictable charge of impairment. It is easier to convict as a recreational user. However, police can impound your vehicle and charge you if they believe you pose a danger on the road whether you are on legal or illegal drugs — or even none at all.

- Some extended insurance will cover — now or in the future — a percentage of your costs of medicines which will include cannabis.

- As a medical user, the cost of setting up a grow room, electrical costs, and ongoing costs (e.g., nutrients and replacement parts) may be tax deductible.

- Your Health Canada-issued document may be recognized by some medical dispensaries in foreign countries and select US states; however, Health Canada states it is not valid outside of Canada.

Just as you would keep any prescription bottle with its label handy in case of any issues when you're going through airport security, for example, whenever you possess cannabis, you will need to carry the container of cannabis you obtained from your chosen LP. It also should have labeled prescription information that validates that you are a legal medical cannabis user. Keeping a picture on your cell phone is good back up.

It is conceivable that each province may bulk purchase its annual medical cannabis consumption to reduce the cost of social medicines.

It is important to note that as a medical user you have certain guaranteed federal rights established by numerous court cases. While the *Cannabis Act* legalizes small amounts of cannabis for adults there are still many issues, constitutional or otherwise, that have yet to be resolved.

Before you apply to Health Canada for a personal or designated production license, you must know in advance where you are going to grow and whether you going to be growing indoors, outdoors, or both. Likely, you won't be able to do both at the same time.

2. Provincial Health-Plan Coverage

Depending on the province, physicians will bill their provincial insurer for signing up patients. There should not be any other fees especially if you a have five-gram or less license. Renewal can be every month or every other year. If there are other fees, you can ask to itemize them in the form of a receipt.

2.1 Qualifying as a medical user

As a result of several court rulings, the Canadian system has strong constitutional requirements that recognize medical cannabis users and provides easy access to their medicine.

Health Canada's current program is called the ACMPR or Access to Cannabis for Medical Purposes Regulations. The ACMPR uses these formulas as part of its guidelines for licensed medical users. I believe the medical program is about one-tenth of the economic size of the recreational market, which tells me it is worth pursuing only if you have a solid business plan.

Here are the Health Canada guidelines for maximum amounts for personal medical use:

- Grams per day x 30 days = maximum amount of personal possession not to exceed 150 g.

- Grams per day x 365 days = maximum amount to be stored at the registered address, if you grow your own plants.

- Health Canada defines a plant as something with a root, a stem, and a leaf.

See Table 4; it indicates sustained and continued growth in the number of legal cannabis consumers.

Statistics Canada will track many data points in an attempt to accurately establish the size of the cannabis industry in Canada. A large portion of the cannabis business is underground but it is estimated to be about $22 billion per year. BC alone is estimated at $6 billion.

Table 4
Growth in Canadian Cannabis Industry

	2014			2015				2016				2017
	Q1	Q2	Q3	Q4	Q1	Q2	Q3	Q4	Q1	Q2	Q3	Q4
1	0.4	0.6	0.8	1	1.3	1.8	2.4	3	4	4.7	5.1	5.8
2	7.9	12.4	15.5	18.5	23.9	30.5	39.6	53.6	75.1	98.4	130	168 [194]

1 kg sold to clients in 1,000s does not include kg produced or in storage or cannabis oil.
2 total number registered users in 1,000s. Fiscal new year April 1.
Source: Health Canada.

To obtain your ACMPR license you must obtain a form signed by a licensed physician. Not all doctors are willing to sign the ACMPR forms due to perceived liabilities associated with medical cannabis. There are many clinics across the country willing to assist including via Skype appointments. Shop around as prices will vary drastically.

Even if your primary care physician is not willing to sign the ACMPR, he or she can find or assist you in finding a qualified doctor that will sign the forms, which includes sending necessary medical documents to the clinic of your choosing.

You should have a clear idea if you are obtaining your personal cannabis from an LP, or if you are going to grow your own plants. You can do both.

If you plan to buy your medicine via LP, the process is quick and you can have your first order within days of registering.

If you plan to grow your own plants, you must be approved by Health Canada first. This process subjects you to Health Canada administrative processes which means approval can take weeks or months. At the time of this writing, there are individuals waiting at least six months for approval. Health Canada is aware that individuals are put in legal jeopardy with expired or near expired licenses and pending renewal applications.

You can obtain cannabis and plant cuttings from an LP even if you are growing your plants.

As a medical user, tax deductions apply to the purchase of medicine and growing equipment. More extended health coverage programs are accepting of cannabis users and several court cases support claims that cannabis is a form of legitimate medicine.

You must keep your personal license current and updated; once you have received your ACMPR you have crossed a legal threshold where you are governed by the ACMPR and not the recreational *Cannabis Act*. I think it is better to be governed under medical rules, especially if you are growing your own as its limits are much higher.

3. The ACMPR's Closed Matrix

In the early days of legal medical cannabis there were a very small number of strains legally available to government-run facilities — usually for the purpose of narcotics control or research. When Prairie Plant Systems (PPS) was awarded the first and sole private production license, the number of strains grew to about 30; however, PPS was constrained by Health Canada and could only offer one strain with a capped potency, ground up (including stem and leaves) and irradiated. This was the only legal source of grown medical cannabis for years and it was terrible, awful looking, and had a poor taste.

When the MMAR was launched in 2001, it also allowed for limited personal production of cannabis, and designated production, using any strain the patient or caregiver could find including from dispensaries or mail-order services. While difficult to calculate, there were thousands of strains in use for many years.

Due to several court cases, MMAR licenses have been grandfathered into existence but exist outside the ACMPR. These grandfathered licenses cannot be modified and cannot be moved to a different address.

When the MMPR came into effect there was a small six-month window in which personal and designated producers could transfer, or sell, their strains to these new corporate entities. Any new strains after this period are off limits to licensed producers.

There is no scientific reason for a closed matrix system.

Newer LPs will have to draw on what the closed matrix can offer a new player. It is unlikely to be a well-tested high-quality choice of strains either in clone or tissue culture option. Something between mid-grade or mediocre is probably what will be available.

The closed matrix also creates a substantial hurdle to small businesses and craft producers entering the legal supply chain. This hurdle has implications for certain chapters in this book such as —

- dispensaries (see Chapter 8), and

- outdoor greenhouse production (see Chapter 10).

4. Applying to Be a Licensed Producer

Applying to the ACMPR to be an LP is currently a very expensive endeavor requiring several highly specialized skills.

Assuming that you have land, or land and building, that you own outright and it complies with municipal zoning then you can expect to spend about $2,000,000 for the application process and then $8,000,000 more to build the approved plans. There will need to be a strong corporate build team to deal with issues related to architecture, engineering, financing, quality assurance, and Health Canada relations. You will also need to assemble a production team once you are licensed (or just prior) which includes genetics and breeding, lights and air conditioning, human resources, financing, plant production/propagation, QA, compliance, maintenance and IT, marketing, etc.

The application process is slow and tedious and it may take years to obtain approval. There are many consultants, including myself, available to guide you through this process if you are still serious about applying to be a Licensed Producer.

Health Canada has divided the application into six parts:

- Intake and Initial Screening

- Detailed Review and Initiation of Security Clearance Process

- Issuance of Licence to Produce

- Introductory Inspection (as cultivation begins)

- Pre-Sales Inspection

- Issuance of Licence to Sell

For more information on applying to be an LP visit healthcanada. gc.ca/mma.

There are a small number of reasons to pursue a medical production license at this point. If your business plan includes a strong IP component in the way of a patentable medical product or a patentable medical device; if you want the ability to import cannabis from abroad yourself versus making an importation agreement with an existing LP; if your goal is to be bought out by a larger organization for substantially more than it cost to set up, then you should consider it.

It is important to note that Health Canada has not licensed any applicants for a distribution-only license or import-export-only license.

Because the federal government has created so many barriers to entry none of the LPs are owned or operated by one or two owners. They are corporately owned with many of them being listed on the stock exchange. This means that mom-and-pop operations should consider applying for micro-production licenses when they become available. Depending on the province, it is possible that the mom-and-pop retail or distribution shop could still exist.

I am of the opinion that if you grow cannabis that passes inspection and analysis, you should be able to wholesale or retail it. The LP's lobbyists will fight you tooth and nail if you voice this opinion loud enough.

If I grow my own tomatoes, I can give some to my neighbor or friends. If I want to sell my tomatoes to a restaurant or the public at large, I should apply to the provincial government to ensure my production facilities meets minimum standards and my product is inspected fairly and randomly for analysis. Food recalls are more common these days and are an important part of keeping the population safe and healthy — if executed in a balanced and fair manner.

In Ontario, omafra.gov.on.ca lays out the process clearly for food producers.

There are several challenges ahead for new and existing LPs; after they pass an arduous approval process, they must keep cost below $2 per gram. The lower the better for obvious reasons, but this has created a race-to-the-bottom culture where the producer can provide the lowest cost product for the highest number of consumers. High-end cannabis is difficult to produce consistently, in large batches, and affordably under an LP environment. Most LPs end up sacrificing high potency for consistency from crop to crop. It may be different for craft producers but it will likely be difficult for them to pocket $5 to $6 per gram net.

Craft producers would be able to compete if the playing field were level; it is currently not level due to the Closed Matrix System and the enormous barriers to entry. Craft producers also face an uphill battle in terms of getting federal approval to produce and distribute cannabis. Some of the unforeseen hazards include cost of compliance and analysis. It is unlikely that a province will be able to authorize producers in the foreseeable future.

Although Canada is leading the global cannabis industry by legalizing cannabis for adult use, other countries are falling in line with a similar commonsense approach to adult use of cannabis. Countries such as Colombia, Jamaica, Costa Rica, and Uruguay are actively working on plans for the legal importation and exportation with Canada of legal cannabis, cannabis products, and genetics. Israel is authorizing many cannabis producers explicitly for the export market.

While every new country that has a compatible cannabis program with Health Canada is good for business in general, the cost of production for South American countries is less than a $1 per gram. As third world countries such as Morocco, Lebanon, and India come on board, the cost of production will be 5 to 25 cents per gram. This long-term strategy further fosters the race-to-the-bottom mentality going on today.

I often wonder how long it will be before cannabis comes to duty-free stores.

5. Health Canada: The Organization

In the context of federal health ministries throughout the world Health Canada must seem like a professionally tightly run efficient agency acting solely in the best interest of the health of its citizens. This may seem true if you were living in an underdeveloped country.

On the surface Health Canada touts its transparency and easy interfacing but a closer look reveals a highly secretive monolithic organization of more than 10,000 staff spread out nationwide. Three executive administrators run its multibillion-dollar budget. It has been called the most secretive government department ("Health Canada Cloaked in Secrecy," *The Globe and Mail*, May 9, 2004); www.theglobeandmail.com/news/national/health-canada-cloaked-in-secrecy/article20433246).

These Health Canada executives earn substantial salaries but the hiring and renewal of these massive employment contracts has no civilian oversight and is highly secretive. Many internal processes and communications are secretive and difficult to access as well.

Health Canada's legal department seems to operate without a budget. In the case of any lawsuit, it does not matter if you are obviously right. It does not matter if it is obvious that Health Canada will lose in court.

If you ever engage in a legal matter with Health Canada, you can expect that it will —

- never settle out of court,

- use every legal opportunity to delay, and

- use every appeal process available.

While I do believe there is no formal blacklist at Health Canada, if you displease Health Canada, which can be very easy to do, you could be informally blacklisted, which makes communications and approvals grind down sometimes as slowly as legally permissible. I recommend treading lightly.

27
Recreational Cannabis in Canada

1. Recreational Users

In Canada, recreational cannabis is governed by the federal *Cannabis Act* (www.documentcloud.org/documents/3565207-Cannabis-Act.html).

Under these regulations cannabis will be legalized for anyone in Canada 18 years of age and older. Each province has jurisdiction to set the age higher than 18 years old, as well as to limit how many plants can be grown at home.

The Act is divided into sections that govern federally regulated issues including:

- Promotions and advertising

- Packaging and labeling

- Selling and distributing

- Ticketable offences

- Licensing and permits

- Tracking and inspections

- Disposal and seizures

- Administrative monetary penalties

- Legislative transitional issues

Although large portions of the Act deal with penalties, minors, and diversion to minors, it does provide a framework for the provinces to take over responsibilities of retail and distribution.

At the time of writing Health Canada has announced its intentions to license micro-producers. This represents the first real attack on the gray and black market by attempting to reduce the costs of entry and red tape to enter the legal market. See Chapter 2 for more about micro-production.

Health Canada is in the process of public consultation and should move to the next phase by the summer of 2018.

This represents a substantial change to the future of cannabis production. As of June 2017, there are almost 7,000 personal or designated production licenses and thousands of unlicensed grow-ops.

It is still not known how many micro-production licenses Health Canada has in mind or will approve. What is the process of approval? Will RCMP security checks be in place? How will micro-producers work with LPs or provincial and territorial partners? As with wineries, will producers be able to sell their products directly to visitors? These are all questions yet to be fully answered.

If you think of the alcohol industry (brewing and distilling), retail and distribution varies from province to province. The criteria each province must decide on how to legalize is what brings in the most provincial revenues for the least effort and which retail and distribution models will best serve the population of that province.

The choice provincial governments must make is whether to have the distribution and retail controlled by the province or by private business or a combination of both.

For the individual adult the *Cannabis Act* will likely allow you, among other things, to —

- grow four plants per household — indoor or outdoor,

- buy, sell, or transfer four non-flowering plants per household,

- possess up to the equivalent of 30g of cannabis and 7.5g of concentrates, and

- transfer up to the equivalent of 30g of cannabis without remuneration.

Note: Corporations are not allowed to possess cannabis.

It is not clear under the *Cannabis Act* if there is a maximum amount of personal storage but it seems similar to a wine, scotch, or cigar collections, in that cannabis has to the potential to have a collectors' value with some consumable items — perhaps packaging as well. An auction of personal collectable cannabis products is unknown to the auction and related industries.

See Table 5 for a chart showing the equivalent of one gram of cannabis and maximum amounts of various cannabis products (these same rules do not apply to ACMPR medical users).

The *Cannabis Act* at time of writing allows for the provinces to be responsible for retail and distribution of cannabis. Each province will have unique demands and will require a new system to meet the needs of that province.

2. Collectibles and High-Value Items

As cannabis use comes into the mainstream, expect a rise in collections of consumable and nonconsumable high-value items. Expect some personal collections to be valued in the high five figures or low six figures. Insurance policies should cover the value of these items in case of theft or fire but make sure your policy explicitly itemizes what you want to insure. Here is a short list of items that could maintain or dramatically increase in value if stored and documented properly:

Table 5
Cannabis Equivalency According to the Cannabis Act

Class of Cannabis	Equivalent to 1g of dried cannabis	30g equivalent
Dried cannabis	1g	30g
Fresh cannabis	5g	150g
Solids containing cannabis	15g	450g
Non-solids containing cannabis	70g	2.1kg
Cannabis solid concentrates	0.25g	7.5g
Cannabis non-solid concentrates	0.25g	7.5g
Cannabis plant seeds	1 seed	30 seeds

Source: The *Cannabis Act*, as of February 2017

- Paraphanelia or accessories with Certificates of Authenticity (COAs).

- Sales receipts from the first cannabis sales with or without attached gram(s).

- Celebrity branded accessories, clothing, musical instruments — or autographed items.

- Commemorative coins with cannabis motifs made in common metals or in pure silver, gold, platinum, palladium, rhodium, etc.

- Glass art and glass marbles, with COA.

- Branded containers.

Alex Grey (www.alexgrey.com) who is a psychedelic artist, identifies strongly with cannabis use for recreational, medicinal, or religious use. His prints and canvases are highly and uniquely detailed as well as very incredibly evocative in nature. They are a worthwhile investment as far as modern art is concerned, especially unique pieces or limited prints with COA. If you have never heard of Alex Grey, I suggest that you pause reading this book, visit his website, consume cannabis if legal in your jurisdiction, and see some of his more popular works. Please resume reading when your mind has been properly blown away. You may want to consume cannabis, again if legal in your jurisdiction, after the experience of being blown away is over or almost over.

Certificates of Authenticity (COA) are issued by the maker or manufacturer as a form of documentation which certifies its provenance (or record of origin or ownership). Some COAs have limited editions with attached serial numbers.

3. Tourists and Non-Canadian Residents and Concierge Services

The *Cannabis Act*, and the Canadian Charter, apply to everyone in Canada — not just Canadians. Mainstream travel packages and concierge services already exist. A small adaptation to their marketing strategy should create several attractive opportunities, and does not require any cannabis-related licensing. Most limousine companies are not smoke friendly; some are vape friendly. Ask ahead of time. Amsterdam had a thriving cannabis tourism industry until Colorado legalized. The lesson learned is that people will travel to Canada just to have a safe enjoyable hassle-free cannabis-related experience.

Creating specialized concierge services for people with extended or long-term visit to Canada could be lucrative. Medical users, for example, could require clinical support, doctor visit(s), transport, accommodations, and specific cannabis products to name a few services. Applicants should send their medical documents ahead of time for approval. They may have to provide an existing Canadian address as part of their applications.

Part 4
US-Specific
Cannabis Business

The following chapters will delve into cannabis issues that are US-specific. If you are looking for Canada-only information please see Part 3.

28
US-Specific Cannabis

1. A Brief History of Legalization in the USA

Legalization of cannabis in the USA has happened by way of voter initiative on a state-by-state basis. The first substantial voter initiative was California's Proposition 215 spearheaded by Dennis Peron who also pioneered retail medical cannabis storefronts, at the time called Cannabis Buyers Clubs.

Billionnaire George Soras was a primary financier of Proposition 215.

Although there have been several such voter initiatives, the next substantial one was Colorado's Amendment 64, which legalized cannabis for adults and allowed for corporate assets to be established. This caused the investment money to pour into the state. Colorado has been a pioneer in corporatized cannabis investment.

The state-by-state voter initiatives puts them at odds with federal government policies, creating arguments of state law versus federal law. Many federal laws and agencies are set up specifically to prosecute and further criminalize any cannabis use and its related business whether legitimate or not.

Even if a business complies with state law, agencies such as the DEA, IRS, and Homeland Security have jurisdiction to prosecute anyone or any corporation doing business in the US.

Tax deductions for cannabis businesses are disallowed and normal banking is near impossible as federal law blocks any attempts at normalization.

Despite these substantial hurdles, Colorado cannabis is a booming business — a testament to the massive and missed business opportunities.

The states/areas where possession for recreational use is legal in some form as of this writing include:

- Alaska
- California
- Colorado
- Maine
- Massachusetts
- Nevada
- Oregon
- Washington
- District of Columbia

Bongs are specifically for cannabis, but water pipes are not specifically for cannabis; American law enforcement takes this difference very seriously and therefore so do retailers. Never use the word "bong" unless cannabis is legal in your state.

One of the organizations to oppose the early criminalization of cannabis/hemp in the 1930s was the newly formed American

Medical Association (AMA), citing cannabis was a reliable ingredient in many approved medicines while cases of cannabis use triggering insanity or murder lacked any merit despite several inquiries by the AMA.

In my opinion, the War on Drugs is one of the reasons race relations and personal rights in the US have deteriorated to the state they are in today. It is also a contributing factor to the increased militarization of law enforcement. In spite of this, every country in the world has successfully imported the American War on Drugs.

A police officer cannot legally harass a person of a certain race simply for standing there. However, as every culture has a relationship to some drugs, criminalizing drugs specific to a culture provides easy, constant opportunities to exploit, subjugate, degrade, and ultimately incarcerate people of that culture. As a consequence, jails have provided substantial sources of ongoing slave labor and continue to do so to this day. The US incarcerates more people per capita than any other country in the world.

Although a clear violation of personal freedoms, Americans in positions of authority or responsibility who require regular urine-based tests willingly set aside their right to privacy and are very much used to submitting to regular drug tests.

Taking a step back from all these facts, we start to see a facet of American national culture. Its core nature is intrinsically and morally opposed to any kind of progressive drug policy. It hates cannabis and everything related to it. There are cultural and legal constructs that prevent individuals who use illegal substances from becoming upwardly mobile.

Legislation, case law, and policies dating many decades support and reinforce oppression and make it difficult to undo for the purpose of legalizing cannabis.

Prohibition has taught us that democracies can be free or drug-free, but you cannot have both.

The documentary *The Culture High* details the early history of American prohibition very well leading up to the 1990s. It draws a clear conclusion that racism formed the basis of our modern prohibition and War on Drugs in the US, which was then exported to Canada and abroad.

The follow-up documentary *The Union: The Business Behind Getting High* explains business details of the underground cannabis economy, specifically in British Columbia.

2. Important Advice for Americans Who Already Have a Cannabis-Related Business

The US government is at least two or three presidents away from legalizing cannabis at the federal level, in my opinion, perhaps more. If you already own a cannabis business in the US, I strongly recommend that you move your business headquarters to Canada as soon as possible. You will then have a Canadian business and recognized corporation with one or more offices in your home state. By doing this you will:

1. Have a cannabis business that is recognized by the federal government and its related agencies: Canada Revenue Agency, Canadian Border Services Agency, and Health Canada to name a few.

2. Any legitimate business you do in Canada is totally and unquestionably legal.

3. Tax deductions are allowable and related expenses are deductible.

4. You have access to the legitimate investment market which could fund your American project. American investors would also be able to invest in your Canadian corporation to fund your offices in the US and elsewhere.

5. Banking is somewhat normalized. The bigger Canadian banks have policies against clients with a cannabis-related business, even if no cannabis is directly involved. There are smaller banks and credit unions that are able to accommodate you.

6. Despite Canadian law, Visa, MasterCard, and several payment gateway systems have strict policies against their use for cannabis-related activities, directly or indirectly. Legal in that jurisdiction or not does not matter to them.

7. Whenever the US does legalize cannabis properly, you can move your headquarters back when it is legal and safe to do so.

8. You cannot launder money with a Canadian account, but you can purchase equipment and pay legitimate bills.

Visit CanadianKushTours.com and select the Business to Business package when you are ready to make a decision. This will not be an easy decision and it may occupy much of your time to accomplish properly.

This is not a search for a better tax plan exactly; this is an escape from substantial persecution. The US federal government has a "cannot do business" attitude. They are programmed to hate cannabis and jail anyone caught associated with it using one of the many mandatory minimum laws available to them. Get some or all of your cannabis business in Canada now. It makes sense from the point of view of removing or lowering the risks of going to jail and having all your assets seized.

29
Medical and Recreational Cannabis in the US

As discussed earlier in this book, there are several enormous barriers to legalizing cannabis in the US for medical or recreational purposes.

Legally referred to as marijuana in the US, cannabis was historically opposed by the alcohol, tobacco, and pharmaceutical lobby (and others). They supported the continued prohibition of cannabis, even if passively. Aside from Norml.org, there was no effort to organize a lobby for legalization until the late 1980s and early 1990s. At that time it was about lobbying for compassionate access to cannabis. There were and are several federal cases in an attempt to legalize medical cannabis with very limited success. It wasn't until Colorado legalized cannabis in 2014 where serious money started going to lobbyists. Once Colorado had several substantial cannabis business success stories, proper lobbying in Washington, DC, was financially possible.

There were many individual efforts made popular, primarily from people facing criminal charges. Organizations such as Law Enforcement Against Prohibition (LEAP) helped in their own way as did many small organizations such as Patients Out of Time.

The lobby effort for legalization is getting easier every day, as polls show that more than 64 percent of Americans agree with legalizing marijuana, and so do 51 percent of polled Republicans (politico.com/story/2017/10/25/poll-americans-support-marijuana-legalization-244155).

It costs a little more than $1 million to launch a basic voter initiative. You must write the proposed legislation that is to be voted on, hire staff to collect the minimum number of signatures of residents of that state, and you must have a minimum number of signatures within each congressional district, and market the proposition leading up to election day. There may be several approvals at the state level to ensure you have met your targets.

Your state will have a written process by which voter initiatives are approved to be on the ballot. There are consultants that specialize in setting up operations for a voter initiative in your state, or neighboring state, who will assist you in this large, multiyear administrative task, if you choose to pursue it. There is no limit to how much you can spend on marketing the proposition.

There are a small number of organizations that oppose legalization such as Smart Answers to Marijuana: SAM and SAM-C in Canada. The website has a decent design template. The information is well laid-out but is somewhat skewed. SAM believes in decriminalizing cannabis only — and not legalization. It favors FDA-approved cannabis-based drugs, but it fails to mention that the DEA must preapprove the study and then the drug approval. Its entire approach to de-penalization would actually strengthen the black market, mostly mom-and-pop shops but not exclusively organized crime. It would also promote thrediscretion of individual police officers regarding whether to lay charges or not. (learnaboutsam. org and learnaboutsam.ca.)

In dealing with any product that is in demand, society is presented with three options:

1. Government controls it.

2. Businesses control it.

3. Criminals control it.

This applies to a wide variety of products and vices. Adding to it is the science stating to treat all drug use as a health issue and that it is counterproductive to criminalize drug addicts and drug users.

As previously stated, in a democracy you can be free or drug-free.

Part 5
Going forward

Now that you have a better idea of your place in the cannabis industry and where you want to end up, make your plans and start consulting other experts in the field you are interested in pursuing. For even more resources to research, see the download kit included with this book. Best of luck with all your endeavors.

30
Summary

Cannabis is still a highly politicized topic. Although countries such as Canada plan to have federally legalized cannabis, and some US states have allowed it, governments come and go and small but important changes to policy can take place that make cannabis consumption easier or more difficult depending on the government of the day.

Things are bound to change, almost daily, for the next while. By the time you read this, links and laws may have changed. Be sure to do thorough research before embarking on any business opportunity.

My hope is that this book has inspired you to tune in, turn on, and help create a truly amazing future for yourself, your family, and your community. Life is too short and too beautiful!

Laughter is a state of grace.

Download Kit

Please enter the URL you see in the box below into a web browser on your computer to access and use the download kit.

| www.self-counsel.com/updates/cannabiz/18kit.htm |

The following files are included on the download kit:

- Questionnaire 1: Insurance
- Questionnaire 2: Should You Grow Your Own?
- Flyer
- Business Plan
- Glossary of Acronyms
- List of Possible Diagnoses
- Resources